Mosaic

Briana Gervat

Apeiron Books

APEIRON BOOKS

ISBN: 978-1542754842

First published in 2017 by Apeiron Books

Printed in the U.S.A.

Memories are mischievous things, often hiding from you when needed most or sneaking up on you when least expected, the trick being to write them down to the best and bravest of your ability, which is what I have attempted to do here sometimes with success and at other times a mistake may have been made recalling the exactness of a conversation or the details of a place, but the intent remains. In some instances names have been changed or omitted depending on the circumstance. In others, friends, having grown bored of their given names, have chosen to go by an alias instead. (Given the choice would you not do the same?) But, for the most part, this is all as it is remembered before it is forgotten.

Like all middle children I blame my parents for all of it: The good. The bad. The downright ugly. I blame them for never saying no. I blame them for showing me all that is good and beautiful and right in this world. I blame them for loving me, even when I did not love myself. But most of all, I blame them for making me believe in love and magic, in mystery and wonder, in resilience and perseverance, without which nothing is possible and with which, everything is possible.

And for Chris, my RHB.

Table of Contents

On Shattered Dreams

On Divorce

On the Best of Summers

On Georgia

On Rwanda

"You have to forget about what other people say; when you're supposed to die, when you're supposed to be lovin'. You have to forget about all these things. You have to go on and be crazy. Craziness is like heaven."

Jimi Hendrix

It is strange, what is remembered and what is forgotten and how memories, once formed, give shape to our lives and all that we are to become.

This is my first memory of the world.

I grew up on an island with the whole of America to the West and to the East, an ocean wider than my imagination and deeper too. Without knowing it, I lived on the edge of the world. Whether it was flat or round did not matter. What mattered was that this land, this solid ground, offered protection from the world beyond. But not always. For sometimes the world likes to remind us of how small we are.

Her name was Gloria. At five I was just tall enough to peer over the ledge of the bay window in our den and watch as the world spun. My younger brother Chris stood to my right and Nick, the oldest of us, stayed close on my left.

Outside, it was light, not yet dark. The clouds above turned from white to gray as they spiraled and whirled across the sky. The boughs of the trees, their leaves still green, creaked and moaned in the howling and wailing wind. How these crowned kings welcomed the madness of the storm and danced in her tempest.

It happened in slow motion and silence. For all too brief of a moment the wind did not know its strength and everything with roots had forgotten their own. One moment it stood, almost alone, the tallest of trees on top of the hill. The next it did not stand at all, but leaned against our neighbor's house; a roof collapsed, a room in ruins. I do not remember being scared watching as this tree crashed down; for these are the moments when fear and reverence are one and the same. I only remember feeling that this hurricane was, at once, more than I will ever be and yet all that I was. Looking back I realize that this, too, was my first lesson in gravity. A lesson that also revealed that things do not always fall down whole: they fracture, they split, they fragment, they shatter. Nothing is permanent.

After, the rain continued to come down in sheets and torrents and then not at all. How still the world became without fury and without sound. Only silence. In the eye of the hurricane my father took us outside to measure the damage that had been done. The earth was cold and wet, but the air was still warm. Autumn had only just begun. I tried my best to leave the twigs where they lie and not step on the acorns shaken too soon from their limbs, but there were too many and they sunk into the sodden earth under the weight of my feet.

So as to not disturb the *Anemoi* from their wakeful rest, we spoke in hushed voices or not at all. If words were said they held no meaning; there was no wind to carry their weight. With the eye of the hurricane above I looked into its pale blue and wondered just how it was possible for the world to be so wild one moment and so tame the next.

When the winds had softened and the clouds had rung the last of their drops from their hold, the sun returned. If it were not for the scattered branches strewn across the yard and a tree that could no longer be climbed the hurricane might have gone unnoticed for the world kept on spinning as if nothing out of the ordinary had taken place. But for a child, for me, this storm was nothing short of extraordinary. Then, as now, I had yet to understand what this world, full of her years and wisdom, understands all too well; that in this life, on this earth, there are squalls and there is stillness, there is chaos and there is calm, there is violence and there is peace.

Of the memories from that room this is but one. There are other memories of teeth lost and Easter eggs found, of watching The Muppet Show and Fraggle Rock, and of listening to Steely Dan and Otis Redding, Tom Petty, Bob Dylan and Roy Orbison (and later, The Traveling Wilburies), over and over again on my father's record player, but those memories were yet to come.

On Christmas Always

And these are my first memories of my world.

I grew up in a house that was never empty, never quiet. Every space held a memory. Every room told a story. But here, it is not the walls that long to tell their tales of all they have seen, all they have heard, and all that they have felt. It is the dishes, the bowls, the forks, and the spoons, for they are the objects that hold all of the warmth and all of the heat of my family within their grasps. In this house the dish would never run away with the spoon; the two of them know better than to do something as silly as that. So, if you listen closely to the dishes, the forks, the bowls, and the spoons, they will tell you of a life that is sometimes sweet and sometimes bitter. They will tell you of a life that is full of love.

This house that was never empty was not only home to my parents, my brothers, and myself, but it was also a second home to anyone else who ever walked through these doors, which included not only my immediate family and all other family members once, twice, and even three times removed, but also all of my mother's best friends from elementary school and high school; friendships which have lasted a lifetime. Her friends became my aunts and uncles, joining the ranks of my aunts and uncles related by blood and their children became my cousins, each of their lives intertwined with our own. And although not all of us are able to trace our sanguinial lines back to one another, our love, like blood, courses through our veins, creating a family without end. And this family, fully extended, does not measure or compare the thickness of blood over water. To us it is all the same. But this strength in numbers did not make us immune to heartbreak; rather it made us more susceptible.

My family descends from strong Polish and Italian stock. Both sides arrived between the wars, when the New Colossus still welcomed people to her shores. From the Old World they brought the traditions of their families that began long before they were born. In the New World they carried them on. Roman Catholic, they raised me to believe in Jesus, Mary, Joseph, the prophets and the saints, Genesis and Revelations. They also raised me to believe in my family, holy in their own right.

This was the way that we celebrated Christmas.

This was the way that we celebrated everything.

In the days before Christmas, when the air stayed cold and snow began to fall, we lit a fire and listened to Bing Crosby's *White Christmas* as we decorated the evergreen tree that stood in our living room. We could not begin until we found THE tape, hidden underneath all the other tapes, and rewind it to whatever song we had to listen to first. Without leaving the living room we traveled around the world. To Ireland we went, to Bethlehem, and even Hawaii too, as we hung ornaments on the tree: delicate blown glass orbs, small ceramic spheres etched with the date of baby's first Christmas, and the newest ornaments, recently constructed in our elementary school art class from multi-colored construction paper and cotton balls fortified with popsicle sticks and then held all together with Elmer's Glue. After the last ornament was hung and Bing sang his last song, we climbed into bed, the scent of fresh pine and sap lingering in the air and the last flames of the fire fading to embers in the cold December night.

On Christmas Eve, in the hours before midnight, we had the Feast of the Seven Fishes. In the oven baked Bakala and shrimp scampi, the butter melting, the garlic roasting, and the parsley, freshly picked from its stems, wilting in the heat. Lobsters, caught that morning in local traps, magically transformed from one color of Christmas to another as the calamari sauce simmered in pots older than me. On the kitchen table there were freselles, pastries, and loaves of bread bought in Brooklyn and the Bronx; all waiting to be broken and shared among us all. In the middle of all of this was found the seafood salad, which was a monstrous bowl full of Mediterranean monsters: scungilli and shrimp swimming in an olive oil sea in which also floated black olives, hot cherry peppers, and crisp celery so thinly sliced that if it were not for its crunch you might have forgotten it was there, which is why if this meal only consisted of this delight alone I would be happy, but this family is Italian and one dish was never enough.

Women of all generations prepared this meal, as they prepared every meal: with love and patience and years upon years of practice. In the kitchen, wearing aprons they had sown themselves, was found my

9

grandmother, Concetta, and her sisters (my greats aunts), Michelina and Filomena, and their daughters: Anita, Diana, and Joanna. And then there was my mother and I. The years had been kind to them and while they may have lost some of their height, they had lost none of their beauty. They were strong women, all of them, who were not afraid to use their voices to speak their minds. And so they spoke loudly and passionately with their hands, their mouths, and their hearts full. The alto of their voices was the sound of Brooklyn before the war and their strength was derived from living through Great Depressions, Great Wars, and great loves, for they were, and always will be, the Greatest Generation. For as long as I could remember I wanted to be one of them without realizing that I already was. There we were, three generations of women in one kitchen, flouring and frying schmeltz, opening the oven to see what was ready to come out, and always stirring the pot in every way possible. And all the while they laughed and smiled and sang to one another as if life were always this simple, this sweet, and this full.

When everything was ready we sat elbow-to-elbow, shoulder-to-shoulder at the table, which was never set for less than twenty, forever bumping into one another, but never being afraid of sitting too close.[1] After all these years, it still surprises me that no one ever got lost in this mayhem and chaos, which might sound impossible when more than a score of family members are squeezed side by side.

Sometimes, from the bench that I shared with my cousin Kristen, I would look down the table, from one end to the other. Being one of the youngest and smallest of children I tried my best to take it all in for it for it

---

[1] Except when it came to sitting next to either of my cousins, Ronnie or Michele, for they were lefties, making it impossible to go just one course without getting elbowed in the ribs, the shoulders, or for those of us little enough, the head.

is a sight to see; thirty people, sometimes more, rarely less, all related by blood, sitting at one table, sharing food and love and laughter. Somehow I had convinced myself that life would always be like this, that time and lives can be suspended and that the people who I loved the most and who loved me right back would always be there, but life is not eternal, only love is.

In between courses all of us children tried to sneak past the adults to do the things that children do, but none of us were ever able to walk by any of our aunts or uncles without being hugged and squeezed and kissed and pinched. Whenever one of us tried to escape from their grasps they only squeezed tighter whispering how much they loved us before finally letting go because time and again, that very same world that reminds us of our smallness, also the likes to reminds us just how big we really are.

At the end of the meal, the men, Sonny and Matty, Johnny and Italo, sat at the far end of the table drinking Campari and sipping espressos while they cut fennel and peeled away the skins of clementines, their hands smelling of citrus and licorice, the scent of strong coffee hanging in the air. These were men who still wore hats when they left their houses and took them off when they entered the homes of others. They held doors open for women and danced like Fred Astaire and sang like Frank Sinatra. They spent what remained of the meal going back and forth between what was remembered and what was forgotten and telling stories of the way things used to be as if they had already began to regret the way things now were and longed for a past that will never be again.

From the din a voice could be heard above all others declaring, "*I am the Great Aunt Fanny!*" Spoken as if she was a magician, or better yet, a witch, a sorcerer, or, at the very least, a teller of fortunes. If there were other great aunts before her I would not know and there has not been one like her since. To her sisters she was Filomena. She was never married and had no great loves to speak of, except her family, which was her first, last, and only love, and for her that seemed to be enough. Her claim to fame was her unwavering belief that my great grandmother put raisins in her meatballs, a fact that her ten brothers and sisters refuted every single time that it was mentioned. How they swore up and down and went blue in the face, until they finally relinquished and told her that she must have had a different mother.

On the Eves that we did not stay at our house and went to my grandparent's house instead, we still celebrated the very same way: with pasta and presents, calamari, or, as we say it in this family, *gallamah*, and gifts.

In the silence of midnight we drove home. My mother in the front with my father at the wheel and the three of us leaning on one another across the backseat searching the December sky for Santa and his eight reindeer, nine on a foggy night, but we never saw him. Our eyes always closed long before we got home.

When day's first light crept through his window, Chris woke up before us all and then woke us up, one by one, to tell us that Santa had indeed been there, that he left presents for all of us, and that he ate the cookies that were left for him and even drank all of the milk that was poured. Still in our pajamas we sat around the tree and shared gifts, some big, some small. And yet, no matter what present I opened, my response was always the same: "*It's just what I always wanted.*"

As we got older and doubt began to creep into our child hearts we noticed that Santa shared the same handwriting as our parents. But that did not matter then, as it does not matter now. All that mattered was that we believed in magic. Then, as now, Christmas and family and magic; to me, they are all the same.

12

On Family

To begin this story in 1980 is to forget the two reasons why this story unfolds as it does: a man and a woman, a husband and wife, a mother and a father. My parents.

Baby boomers, my parents were born in the years between the end of the Second Great War and the beginning of the Cold War, when America was in flux and all that had been learned had been forgotten. They, too, were born on this island, much different then than it is now.

Sometimes I like to imagine them as the children they once were rather than the adults they are now. In other words, I like to imagine THEM before US and this is what I imagine:

I imagine how they must have smiled when they heard Rock n' Roll for the first time. How my mother must have screamed and shouted when the British Invaded for the second time, this time with mop-tops instead of wigs and guitars instead of bayonets. I imagine how scared they must have been in the early years of the McCarthy Era and then, later, how terrified they must have been when the Vietnam War had begun. How they must have cried on those tragic days when they learned that John F. Kennedy had been shot, when Martin Luther King was shot, and when Robert Kennedy was shot. How full of wonder they must have been when a man walked on the moon. How full of gratitude they must have been when the Paris Peace Accords were signed. How young they must have been.

My father is a carpenter, a philosopher, a scientist, a part-time Republican, and a daydreamer. My father is also Polish, but he does not descend from those whom jokes are made at their expense, but from a people who are poets, revolutionaries, composers, and scientists, and it must be said that my father can change a light bulb all by himself. He stands just two and a half inches below six feet. Most days he is quiet, absorbed as he is in his own thoughts, but some days, when he feels like it, he will talk about everything, as long as you don't mind hearing the same story twice. But those occasions are rare. At sixty-six he still has a full head of brown hair with few grey hairs of which to speak and aside from the pounds he has gained over the years he does not look much different from the day I was born.

My mother, a full-blooded Italian woman with dark brown hair and dark brown eyes, is full of passion and vulnerability, stubbornness and compassion, fury and fervor; after all, she is a Gemini. She is also one of fifty-two first cousins, which only demonstrates that Italian and Catholic are two words never to be separated. Like many women born in her family, she was expected to follow the traditions of her mother and her mother's mother before: marriage and soon after, children of her own. This was a fate that my mother willingly accepted for family is where she finds all of her strength.

Mary Michele Chirichella Gervat will be the first to tell you that her legs are too skinny and maybe even that her boobs are too big, but if you ask me, it is her heart that is too big, or just big enough to hold all that life has asked from her and then some. Styles may have waned and waxed since 1950, but she is and always has been one classy bitch. She loves to sing, sometimes off key and mostly out of tune, but she sure can mash potato better than anyone I have ever known. At sixty-five, or as she likes to call it these days, 'sexy-five,' my mother is the same height that she has been for the last fifty years. Unlike her mother and her aunts, my mother has yet to shrink. She only continues to grow.

My father grew up in Albertson, New York, the son of Polish immigrants. My grandmother, Stascha was born in Buffalo. Not long after, her mother took her back to Poland where she stayed until the spring of 1939, just weeks before the Germans unleashed the blitzkrieg across her native land beginning yet another war on the continent.

When she was nineteen she returned to America and worked as a domestic in Florida where she learned to speak English and drive a car. In 1945, she married my grandfather, recently returned from the theater of war in the Far East. Three years later my father was born on the fifth of October. The middle of three children, he is the only boy among girls. He was given the name John Dennis Gervat. John after his father and Dennis, not after the Patron Saint of Paris who protects against frenzy, strife, headaches, hydrophobia, and possessed people- although in many ways my father does all of these things- but perhaps simply because she liked the name. To differentiate between husband and son my grandmother took to calling him Denny in her still thick Polish accent laden with Old World charm, but his friends thought she was calling him Danny so they did too and the name stuck.

Whether extremely pious or grossly heretical, my father spent his youth reenacting scenes from the Bible with his friends (and sometimes apostles) in his backyard. Over the course of elementary school they worked their way through the Old Testament and into the New. When it came time to perform the Crucifixion, he was chosen to play Jesus, while his friends, the modern day Roman guard, fixed him to poorly constructed scraps of two-by-fours, more two than four, and raised the cross, which quickly fell with astonishing, yet inevitable speed to the ground. Unable to wait the prescribed three days to rise he ran immediately into the bathroom, knees bleeding and face scratched, and got the biggest bandages he could find: his mother's Kotex. In this instant my father displayed a delightful combination of obliviousness and ingenuity that, like the scars he received that day, would stay with him for the rest of his life.

When he was sixteen, his father died from complications of alcoholism. As a child he had watched his father unravel one day at a time, one drink at a time and yet, if and when he ever speaks of him, it is the always sober moments that he recalls. After the death of his father, my father invested all of himself into sports. He found wrestling where, on and off the mat, he grappled with opponents' real or imagined and even after season had ended and well after his boots had been hung up, he spent the rest of his life wrestling a past that he could never entirely overcome. When he was not in the ring my father surfed and most mornings he could be found floating in the ocean on a fiberglass board coated in resin with only one fin and without a leash.

Somehow, someway my father learned how to walk on water.

My mother was born in Brooklyn on June 4, 1950, the daughter of Matthew Chirichella and Concetta Maria Viola. Her parents, Connie and Matty met and fell in love long before December 1941. After the attack on Pearl Harbor, Matty was sent to the war in the Pacific, where he stayed until 1945. In the last weeks of the war he loaded the bombs that were later dropped on Hiroshima and Nagasaki before returning to New York as Japan mourned their dead and prayed for peace. There are those that say that he returned to America a hero, but really, he returned home as a twenty-two year old boy who had seen enough of war that peace, real peace, evaded him for the rest of his life.

When he returned to the neighborhood where he grew up after four years of war Matty married his sweetheart and together they moved from Brooklyn to the suburbs where they bought a three-bedroom house with a fully finished basement and a backyard, just for the two of them and their family to be; so very different from the railroad car apartments they grew up in. Soon after, they had two children, a boy, John, and a girl, my mother. Like most firstborn girls of the Viola-Chirichella clan she was named Mary Michele. Always strong of will and never liking the name she was given she, too, went by her middle name.

Small wonder that my mother and father wound up together;
They were meant to be.

Although they attended the same high school my mother and father did not meet until the summer of 1966. My mother was too busy solidifying her reign as the class flirt and my father contenting himself with dating all of the women who were not my mother. But on that August day they went to the beach, they fell in love, and I would like to believe that they have been in love ever since.

For college, my father went to Fort Schuyler where he studied economics and marine transportation and became a merchant marine. He spent the remaining years of his youth on ships exploring the high seas, a pirate born a century too late.

His journeys took him far away from New York and far away from my mother, but no matter where he was he always wrote her page after page of love letters, a stack of which she still keeps bound with string in the drawer of the night table next to their bed.

When he returned from sea he married my mother on her twenty-second birthday. My mother wore a brocaded dress made by her mother and my father a tuxedo so quintessentially 1972 that he has not worn it since. They ate cake and danced to the Beatles. They were happy. They were in love. For their honeymoon they went to the South of France and Switzerland and when they returned my father began a business manufacturing harness horse racing equipment; chariots of the twentieth century. Together they bought a house twenty-seven miles from where they grew up in a town without sidewalks and within walking distance of the beach. It was another county, another world. But they were young and they had their whole lives ahead of them.

For years they tried to have children, but try as they might they could not. Most nights, my mother fervently prayed to her God, offering the roof over her head and the shirt off of her back if only He would bless her with children.

Silly woman. She did not yet know for what she asked.

Finally, when all of her prayers seemed to fail- perhaps the gods were not listening- they conceded defeat and decided to adopt. My brother Nick was born on August 14, 1978. Three days later they took him home and unwrapped him like a gift on the couch in the den. They counted his fingers, they counted his toes, and, most of all, they counted their blessings. How they cooed and sang him sweet lullabies, forgetting once and for all how long it took them to get from there to here. In that moment he was perfect and he was theirs. Two years later my mother learned that she was pregnant, a seemingly impossible feat, and yet, an ordinary miracle. I arrived after sixteen hours of labor- a fact that my mother loves to remind me of on the days that I continue to be a pain in her a**- and my brother Chris just sixteen months after that. Then there were five of us: Danny and Michele, Nick, Brie, and Chris.

Perhaps prayers, like light, bend and refract
as they travel through the heavens,
forever altering their paths, but always returning as light nevertheless.

My father's business took him to the far reaches of Western Pennsylvania, the blue hills of Kentucky, and the not so distant horse farms of New Jersey. Whether he was gone for a day or a week, he always found us waiting for him at the top of the stairs when he returned, ready for him to spin us around on the hardwood kitchen floor; a tradition that began who knows how or when, but continued until we had grown too big or perhaps it was only the floor had grown too small. As we spun we shrieked and laughed and begged him for more no matter how dizzy we became, but he never stopped; egged on as he was by our endless enthusiasm for centripetal forces. Spinning around and around and around on the oak wood floor we learned to always seek the center, the heart of the matter and nothing else. And, without anything to hold onto, we also learned how to let go.

At night, when the world grew quiet and my eyes grew sleepy, my father lured me to the *Land of Nod* with stories of all the adventures he had before I was born. He told tales of distant cities, faraway lands, and peregrine people. He spoke the Straights of Gibraltar. He whispered of Halong Bay. He sang of Rembrandt. Of his journeys there are but few photographs, choosing instead to capture the moments in his mind rather than on film and to this day he can still close his eyes and remember everything; as if the only time that has passed was the blink of an eye.

Most nights, my father knelt by the edge of my bed, leaning in to share with me the stories of his life:

"Did I ever tell you about the time that I lived in Hawaii…"
"Yes, Dad, but can you tell me again?"

"What about when I was in the Philippines?"

"What were you doing in the Philippines? Where are the Philippines?"

"What about the time that we went surfing in the Outer Banks?"

"Which time?"

"The time where we drove all the way down Route 1 and then followed the swell up the coast."

"Can we do that one day?!?"

"Of course we can."

But my favorite story was not of Hawaii or the Outer Banks. It was of no place in particular and still the only place I wanted to be, for my father's stories of land were nothing compared to his stories of the sea. And so I held my breath and listened with eyes wide opened, not willing to miss a single word as he told me about what it was like to be on the biggest of ships in the middle of the widest of oceans:

As a lieutenant, it was my duty to stand watch on the deck of a ship. On nights when there was no moon and there were no clouds only the sound of the engine could be heard in the darkness. Everything was quiet. Everyone was asleep, except for the stars that sprawled across the endless sky. There were more than I could count and more than I could name so I stopped trying to count them and I stopped trying to name them and just sat there in the silence while the whole of the universe spun around me.

It was only when he finished that I closed my eyes, not to sleep, but to imagine myself there, alone on a ship with only the heavens above, forever shining even in the darkest of nights. If and when I finally fell asleep, for sleep does not come easy for those who dream, I dreamt of oceans, I dreamt of stars, I dreamt of the sea.

From my father I inherited wanderlust and a restless soul; for once you become aware of motion, whether it is the movement of the waves, the wind, or the world, it is difficult to stand still.

My mother is also a storyteller. Her voice is raspy and deep, her words rhythmic and full of soul. At all times of day she shared both stories of her childhood and stories that were not her own. Just before sleep, she read to me from hardbound books with worn pages and colorful illustrations of secret gardens and the littlest of princesses. When I was not reading, I held these books to my heart- even though they were already there- or up to my nose to breathe in their scent, sometimes old and musty, sometimes new and sweet, like the way a pitcher, standing all-alone on the mound, smells his glove before releasing his first perfect pitch.

From my mother I have inherited a love of books and stories, real and imagined. Did my mother know what she was doing? Was it part of her plan to foster a love of something that could never and would never cease? I'd like to think so. But she must also have known, too, that books are dangerous things for books are combustible; not only because their pages are made of paper, but also because they ignite our imaginations, leading all of us to believe that maybe, just maybe, there are portals in the least likely of places that transport us to lands near and far, where boys can indeed fly, where animals do indeed speak, where trees just might come to life, and girls can become anything and everything they please. At least that is what books, the best kinds of books, have done for me and in the years that followed, books became an escape, a place to travel when there seemed as if there was nowhere else to go.

My mother also shares the same adventurous spirit as my father, but it is not at the helm of a ship that my mother is most confident. It is the wheel of a car that draws my mother to the road. On days without school my mother took us into the city. We drove over bridges and through tunnels, trading one island for another. On the edge of Queens a landscape of mountains made by men rose up across the river. New York City. No matter how many times we travelled these roads it was always as if we were seeing this city for the first time; a view that has yet to grow old, despite all of the years that have passed from then until now.

Once in Manhattan, we parked downtown and rode an elevator up 1,310 feet, 107 floors to the observation deck of the South Tower of the World Trade Center. How fast it climbed. How dizzy we were from ascending so quickly. But that did not stop us once the elevator doors opened from running to the windows and pressing our hands and faces against the glass to look down to the ground below, all the while shouting for everyone to hear, "*Look ma! Ants!*" Everything looked so small, everything moved so slowly and all around us stood the monuments of the New World: the Statue of Liberty, the Empire State Building, the Brooklyn Bridge, but here, in this place, we stood on top of the world. How big we were in that moment. How invincible. How unconquerable. From those days on, these towers became my New York, my pharos, my lodestars, forever letting me know that I was home. After we left the city I always, always, always looked back just to make sure they were still there.

On the Beach

To grow up on an island is to be surrounded by water and this island, long and narrow, carved by the sea is shaped like a fish. How could it not be so that we who inhabit this land, too, are carved from its waters?

Unable to sever ties with ships or the sea my father bought boats: speed boats and motorboats, all engine and no sails. So our summers were spent off the coast where the Long Island Sound aspires to join the Atlantic Ocean. In this place where everything moves and nothing stands still, these boats became islands all our own.

He named our last boat *THE FIV OF US* as a tribute to the immediacy of his family. In warmer longer days we left the dock of the marina and sought the waters of the continental shelf. Off the stern we dropped anchor and Chris, Nick, and I climbed up to the top of the deck and jumped into the water below, always daring each other to jump higher and higher and further and further, forever fearless, forever free. Even with pruned skin and chattering teeth we refused to get out of the water, which never mattered to our parents because this was their day just as much as it was ours and they, too, were here to stay.

From the deck of the boat came the sound of what was to become the soundtrack of my childhood echoing across Sound. The year was 1986. The album was *Graceland*, and this album not only defined the sixth year of my life, but every year thereafter, and from the water my brothers made the sign of the teaspoon while the sea made the sign of the wave.

At night, when the world grew silent, but never still, and even the wild osprey laid down to rest in their nests on high, we were rocked to sleep by wave after wave lapping against the hull making the ocean my first lullaby drawing me into dreams big and small.

On the North Fork of the East End of Long Island there is a small town called East Marion where my parents rented a house each summer. It was only for a week, sometimes two, and yet it seemed like our whole summer was spent out there. After all, what is time to a child but a magnification of infinity?

This house, like our own, was never empty. With seven rooms and steps that led down to the beach and doors that were always open, it was hard for anyone to stay away. Besides, everyone was always invited. And so they arrived with beach chairs and bathing suits to revel in the never-ending delights of summer. Here, everyday was an adventure. Every night was a feast.

As children, we ran barefoot along the wild coast. Whether it was just the three of us or all of our cousins, blood related or otherwise, we skipped stones flattened by the persistence of time, picked up horseshoe crabs by their telsons, and searched for Indian arrowheads among the discarded and shattered shells of the shore.

Despite the lack of waves, my father brought with him his surfboard to be used as a slide on which he placed each of us, one by one, or sometimes two at a time, on the back of the board before lifting it over his head so we could glide down into the water. It never occurred to us in these perfect moments that one day we would grow too big for these childhood pleasures. When it rained we stayed inside and played UNO, spoons, and hide and go seek in the hallway without end, peeking into each and every one of the nine doors hoping to find whoever it was or whatever it was we were looking for.

When night returned with its mysteries and the fireflies glowed soft and low in the growing darkness, we shucked corn plucked just hours before from the farm down the road and raced lobsters across the linoleum floor, the string from the corn still sticking to our arms and legs and the rubber bands still wrapped around the claws of the lobsters. In our innocent cruelty we granted the winning lobster a few more moments of freedom before dropping him into the water that boiled on the stove and then served him and his opponents for dinner, cracking their shells open and dipping the warm white meat into a post mortem victory bath of butter.

When there was no more lobster to be had, we went back outside in search of more adventures in the night. From the deck of our borrowed house we watched as first the bright queen of the sky appeared on the horizon and then as a man appeared in the moon. In the darkness, we climbed onto the wooden rails, sun bleached and salt dried, and traced our fingers around big bears and little bears, lions and planets near and far. During the Perseids we held our hands up to the sky hoping to catch just one of the passing meteors before they disappeared until the following summer. When stars fell we made wishes never caring whether or not they came true as the tide came and went in the water below.

And yet, not every memory of the beach is filled with sunshine and rainbows. For there are some days when the sun disappears behind gathering clouds and shadows are cast, if only for a moment.

Forever defiant and desperate for independence-even at four- I never listened when I was told what to do and what not to do, especially when it came to the water. So on that dog day, out I walked into the harbor, to the place beyond where my feet could touch the ground and the place where the currents move not towards, but away from the shore.

From the shore my mother counted: six little boys, five little girls, six little boys, five little girls. Had I known that she was counting, had I cared, I would not have gone from floating one moment to sinking the next. And yet, I did not scream. I did not call out. I only watched in silence as the gulls traced unknown patterns in the sky. And then, there was darkness. *Six little boys, four little girls.*

Underwater her scream could not be heard, but how it must have pierced the air. For an eternity my mother cried out my name as she ran towards where I remained submerged.

From the day we are given life, far from death we never stray.

Just as my body began its final descent into the blue, hands and arms wrapped around me. A teenager, no more than fifteen, moved quickly when everything and everyone else stood still. He pulled me out from the depths and brought me back onto dry land before all air escaped from my body and water filled my lungs. We never caught his name or where he was from but whoever you are and wherever you may be, thank you. A million times thank you for saving my life. Thank you for rescuing me from the currents and returning me to my family. Thank you for bringing me back to my mother. Thank you. Thank you. Thank you. Thank you.

There are no certainties in this life except perhaps one:
There are, indeed, angels among us.

And still, despite this almost sacrificial offering of myself, I return to the beach over and over again because in this littoral life where everything is ephemeral and nothing is permanent, sand gives way, water recedes and advances, we emerge and return from whence we came.

For it is only here, at the beach, among these fragments of sand and rocks, that I am whole. And on this island, in this tidal silence, I stand at ease along the edges of the earth, telling the sea my secrets and whispering my dreams to the wind, whereupon, the vastness of the sea swallows each and every one of these dreams and has since returned them to me in waves of a particular order.

Backyards: those places full of trees begging to be climbed and swings longing to be swung. If ever, as kids, we were inside it was because the rains came down too heavy or because the hour had grown too late, otherwise outside was where we were to be found exploring our world and laying claim to what was ours however temporarily borrowed from the earth that it was. More often than not it was just Chris and I in the yard and not always Nick because throughout this life there has rarely been a time when

Nick and I got along for more than a few moments. With us, it has always been a battle, one which neither of us has ever won.

But for Chris and I, our battles were different: less volatile, more definitive. In constant competition, our backyard became our arena, our stadium, and our colosseum, where we raced each other from one end of the yard to the other, we played baseball and basketball, and learned at a very young age that we were and always will be athletes. As the years grew longer, Chris grew taller, a feat that I never forgave my little brother for. But then again it never mattered what heights he grew to, I have always looked up to him.

For hours, Chris and I built forts made of snow in the winter and sticks in the summer. We played manhunt, capture the flag, freeze tag, and every other tag imaginable. We took turns pulling the sulkies designed by our father, one of us the horse, the other the jockey, and raced around the *Circus Maximus* of our backyard. When we were not on the sulky, we swung on the hammock that hangs between the two oak trees that stand the perfect distance apart from one another. Reckless and daring, we pushed each other higher and higher to see, even if we flipped over, if we could still hold on. If we did not fall face first into the dirt and rocks below, there we were, tangled in a web of rope and wood shrieking with laughter and saying to one another: "*I bet you can't do that again*," bets that we continued to win for what remained of our childhood.

At the edge of the woods there was a swing set where we became monkeys or trapeze artists, more upside down than right side up. When the yard was not enough we roamed the acres of woods behind our house until it grew dark. A bamboo forest became our fortress where we stumbled upon fossils of the Holocene epoch: the skulls of foxes, the shells of eastern box turtles, and the shedded skins of garter snakes. To our backyard we returned

34

triumphantly with our trophies wondering what it was that we might find next time in our wilderness.

Despite all of this I escaped childhood unscathed. No broken bones of which to speak, no stitches sewn, no scars that told stories all their own. There were only the occasional scrapes and bruises, cuts and scratches, and my body's vehement reaction to the shining leaves of poison ivy that I knew better not to touch, but touched nevertheless.

Of course throughout this childhood of mine there were other seasons and other memories. In the winter there were mountains covered in snow and toboggan runs built by my father on the hill in front of our house. In the fall there were soccer games as the leaves turned from green to orange to yellow and when those leaves fell, they were gathered into piles and jumped into when the ground was closer and gravity meant less. And in the spring there were the crocuses that fought their way through the last of the frost whispering of the warmth to come.

But even in the winter, even in the spring, even in the fall it is always summer. For summer is a time for watermelon, a time for hammocks, a time for thunder, a time for lightening, and a time for magic.

If not in Northport or at the beach, we were in Mineola at my grandparent's house, which was a cape with three bedrooms, two bathrooms, and a fenced in backyard. My grandmother, her hair silvered and peppered by time, waited for us at the door, ready to shower us with kisses and food. In her kitchen, she fried meatballs made from pork, veal, and beef ground that morning by the butcher, she scrambled peppers and eggs, and when she did not feel like cooking she made us bologna and cheese sandwiches on

Portuguese rolls still warm and soft from the bakery.

We sat at the table unable to get up until our plates were clean and our bellies were full because my grandmother was never able to overcome the scarcity of the rationing that she had experienced during the war and perhaps she remained uncomfortable with ideas of abundance and waste and still lived in great fear that one day the stock market might crash again and another war might begin.

On her refrigerator there were lessons, sometimes typed, sometimes handwritten, and sometimes clipped from the pages of Reader's Digest; lessons that were only able to be learned in her kitchen:

"If you say what you think, don't expect to hear only what you like."

"You can please some of the people most of the time and most of the people some of the time, but you cannot please all people all the time."

And then there was my grandmother's personal philosophy of all things karmic:

"You spit up in the air it comes down in your face."

My grandfather was a proud man who convinced himself, and all of us, that he was over six feet tall. By the time that I was born little remained of his hair and he wore a toupee to cover what had been lost, but no matter the toll that time had taken on his head he was still one of the most handsome men I have ever known. Taking great pride in the small strip of land he was able to call his own, he kept the grass in front of his house perfectly manicured. There was never a stray blade to be found, never a fallen leaf that remained long on the ground. Whenever we came too close, his voice boomed from a place unseen and unknown: *"Get off the lawn!"* And off we scattered, afraid of what might happen if he found us on his lawn again. After all, why play on the veritable safety of the lawn when there was a perfectly unsafe abandoned parking lot full of broken glass and gravel and

36

weeds right next to his house?

My father's mother, Stella or Stascha, depending on which version of her name she chose to go by, cooked for us too, mostly from scratch and rarely without butter. In our kitchen or her own she prepared breakfasts of pancakes with homemade applesauce made from thinly sliced apples laden with powdered cinnamon, melting butter, and granulated sugar left to simmer on the back burner until the mixture turned soft and sweet. If she woke up early enough after the nights she slept over she made cheese blintzes filled to the brim with farmer's cheese and topped with raspberry jam and for dinner there was always meatloaf with canned peas or pirogues with onions sautéed brown and crisp.

As we ate, she sat at the kitchen table and smiled and laughed, perhaps knowing something or everything that we did not. She, too, never forgot the war and the sacrifices that were made so when it came time for our baths she only filled the tub to the tops of our feet and the water grew cold long before we were clean, but given the choice between the cool of the water or the warmth of her love I would choose her over and over again.

Barely a memory of my grandparents is one without food for this was the way they shared their love with their children and their children's children and their love was as tangible as the meals we ate: rich and warm and always more than a little leftover.

So many days were spent like this, but looking back there were not enough. Not. Even. Close.

On Death and Other Demons

Born in 1980, I am a child of the eighties: not quite part of Generation X and definitely not a millennial. So perhaps those of us born within those few years can consider ourselves Inbetweeners or the Last Generation: in between what was and what is and the last generation to grow up without and to come of age with the now conveniences of the modern age.

In this generation there was no Facebook of which to speak, no iPhone, no iPod, and definitely no iPad. If answers were sought, they were found by asking real people or looking in encyclopedias, real encyclopedias, bound in leather, because then, google was only a number and not yet a verb. For the first two decades of my life, quarters were still kept in pockets so that phone calls could be made and the only person we knew to have a cell phone was Zach Morris. This was a time when MTV still played music videos and innocence lingered well into our teenage years. We were a generation on the verge: the end of one millennia and the beginning of another.

And these years, this decade, was the best time to be a young girl because we grew up believing that we could be anything and that we can do everything. Everything that our mothers fought for and their mothers before them were no longer dreams but real, actual possibilities, and equality was finally almost within our grasps. We could play sports like Billie Jean King, go into space like Sally Ride, and maybe even one day become the President of the United States of America.

And yet, despite all of these hopeful promises, this world was full of constant threat. In countries near and far there were revolutions. All across America there was homelessness. There were holes in the ozone layer. There was acid rain. And let us not forget about the Cold War. For years, we stood on the edge of brinksmanship, as if the whole world held their breath waiting for another war to end all wars to begin. And then there was AIDS. In those early years of the epidemic, AIDS was a disease for which there was no cure and still no explanation. For a child, for me, all of this was beyond comprehension. And so for an entire decade I lived in hope and I lived in fear of a world I was still too young to understand afraid to ask the questions that lingered on all of our lips:

Was another atomic bomb to be dropped?
If I touched someone, if I hugged someone, if I kissed someone, would I get HIV?
Would it become AIDS? Would I die?
Could I be president one day?
Was a woman to be president some day?
What was the future going to be like?
Was there going to be a future?

On and on these questions raged, almost always going unanswered and during these years these hese fears became more real than any monster that might have been in my closet and scarier than any nightmares that I may have had in the dark. When I began kindergarten these fears of the world at large hung in delicate balance with my own childish fears, but it was fear

42

mingled with hope and it was with this hope that I began kindergarten and it was in kindergarten that I met them.

In Mr. Milau's class, a room full of Lincoln Logs, Fisher-Price cash registers, and even a seesaw, we sat together, sharing our small table with the only boy in our grade who did not have koodies. Thereafter, it was always the three of us: Melissa, Amanda, and Briana. I do not remember having any other friends before Amanda and Melissa and I never imagined myself needing any other friends besides them.

Even though we were all so different, we remained inseparable from the day we met. At five, Amanda was tall with blond hair and blue eyes and a mischievous smile that has yet to fade. Melissa was the opposite with olive skin and eyes so green that they constantly changed in the light and her curly brown hair never obeyed any laws, not even her own.

The fates foretold of our friendship long before we were born for we were already connected, for even friendship has its string theories, ways in which we are bound to one another by sometimes visible, sometimes invisible threads of life. This was our theory:

In Mineola, my mother and Amanda's father, Doug, grew up one block away from one another. Years later, they crossed paths again in an aisle of the A+P where they soon discovered that they were neighbors once more. Melissa's father, Sonny, and my Uncle Jimmy- my father's best friend from high school- were roommates in college and now all of our families lived less than one mile apart. Small Island. Small world.

Of my memories from those innocent days there are but few that Melissa and Amanda were not a part of. Always outside, never in, we played soccer and basketball, we swam and rode bikes, and we swung on swings, kicking our legs out into the sky and just for that moment we knew what it was like to fly. At the end of October, we paraded around the parking lot of

43

Bellerose Avenue Elementary School in our Halloween costumes: Amanda as Jem, Melissa as a cheerleader, and me as Punky Brewster. After, we went trick-or-treating until our pillowcases were full and the last light of the once warm sun disappeared behind the trees. There were very few weekends that were not spent sleeping over each other's houses only to stay up all night talking about all of the boys that we had crushes on and all of the things that we were going to do together when we grew up because we were always going to be together. Always.

Time passed and Kindergarten became first grade and first grade turned into second grade and our friendship turned into a thing of magic. A tree house became our sanctuary. Accessible only by a trap door and a secret password, it stood high off the ground, with wooden walls that rose up taller than the tallest of us. On a bench hidden from view we laughed and made up only one word, which meant nothing and everything all at once and, when whispered, seemed to say what every other word in every other language could not. This single word came to define our friendship:

Fatchacoti. Fatchacoti. Fatchacoti.

Since both Amanda and Melissa had in-ground pools in their backyards, complete with slides and diving boards, we spent our summers splashing and shouting, *Marco, Polo*, or keeping as quiet as possible so that no one would ever know that there was a fish out of water. In those dog days we only got out if thunder was heard and lightening was seen and even then, we waited until the first drops of rain fell into the pool creating tiny ripples of water that collided with one another creating infinite circles across the already wet surface.

The summer between second and third grade was the summer we tried to perfect our diving skills. Ever fearless, Amanda and I dove head first into the water, sometimes backwards, and sometimes even flipping over, trying our best not to land on our backs or our stomachs. Melissa followed us with cannonballs and belly flops even when we dared her, double dared her, and even triple dog dared her to dive in with her arms over her head.

"Come on Melissa. You can do it!" We shouted to her as we treaded water in the deep end. But she always jumped in feet first telling us that it hurt her neck to try it any other way. Long after we had become prunes, we dried ourselves off, never giving it a second thought.

When summer ended, as summer does, we returned to school to begin third grade. On Columbus Day Weekend, 1988, our families went to Montauk to revel in the last of warm days and yet, on that October day, there were no sun, only the darkest of clouds, a wind without cease, and a restless sea, in other words, the perfect day for Melissa and I to play chicken with the ocean. At eight, we thought ourselves to be bigger than the waves and maybe even the world and, maybe, just maybe, that day, we were. But we went too close or too far or did not come back soon enough. That was when the ocean knocked us down, soaking our jackets and our pants, our sneakers and our socks. Nothing was dry. Everything was wet. Water filled my ears, sand filled my sweater, tears filled my eyes, and I did not need to hear or see my mother to know how much trouble we were in.

That night the Melissa and her family did not come with us to dinner. Melissa was sick. She had come down with a cold, but colds are supposed to go away. They are not supposed to last for weeks. Colds are common. They are not rare like the rarest of cancers.

In November, they diagnosed her with Chordoma, "a rare and cancerous tumor that can occur anywhere along the spine, from the base of the skull to the tailbone." It was not fear that held Melissa back from diving into her swimming pool. It was a tumor, which had nestled itself somewhere along her thoracic spine, somewhere between her present and her future. According to the Chordoma Foundation, Chordoma's are generally slow growing, but relentless and tend to recur after treatment. Forever a warrior, she underwent chemotherapy nevertheless.

Because of her diagnosis Melissa missed most of the third grade and her chair remained on top of her empty desk. Sometime before the winter holiday, Melissa walked into Mrs. Murphy's classroom. But there she could not stay. She could not even take down her chair. She wanted so badly to remain where she was that she began to cry. I did too. Maybe we all did. Maybe all of us there in Mrs. Murphy's class, eight year olds who knew nothing of long division or cursive or even why the world was round, did not know what to do as we watched our friend leave with her father, never to return.

After that, everything changed. Instead of playing soccer or Tutti Frutti, we stayed inside her house and played Nintendo and we played Monopoly, letting her pass go, letting her get out of jail free, and letting her do whatever the hell she damn well pleased.

Time passed and her cancer progressed, spreading down her spinal column from her Atlas to her sacrum. Relentless and slow growing. Slow growing and relentless.

Progress. What an awful word for dying.

Over the winter Melissa was taken to a specialist in Boston, where Amanda and I visited her in the hospital. Outside it snowed and in their furor and frenzy the flakes made one last leap into the cold January air before covering the ground in white. Inside it was dark, the lights low, and the room quiet. We crept quietly over to the place where Melissa lay asleep in her bed. By then she was paralyzed, her neck braced with metal rods that extended over her head holding it in place. A metallic halo. Another angel in our midst.

When they brought her home, our best friend, who ran the Great Cow Harbor Race and stood up against the sea, could no longer move and she could no longer speak. And if she could, what would she have said? For us, it did not matter. Words were no longer necessary.

Thereafter, the den became her bedroom. The place where Amanda and I read to her from *Highlights* magazine and convinced her that she did not miss anything in third grade, that boys still had koodies, and that this time with just the three of us was more fun than school ever was and ever will be. After all, ideas of death do not enter into the imagination of children.

That day was the day Melissa turned nine. Weeks passed and then months and then it was August.

What I remember of Wednesday, August 9, 1989:

The sun shining.
The phone ringing.
The door opening.
Two words repeated over and over and over again.
"*She's gone. She's gone. She's gone*"
47

My mother holding me, refusing to let me go.

Tears, oh so many tears.

Still in my bed, I wanted to believe that it was all a dream. I wanted to scream and tell my mother that she was a liar because I could not believe, would not to believe that she was telling the truth; that Melissa was dead, that my best friend was gone. But I did not scream. I did not call my mother a liar. I did not say anything at all. I only stayed in bed and my mother stayed with me. She never let me go.

What I wish I could forget about August 9, 1989:

Everything.

I mourned her death in the only way that a nine year old who knew nothing of death can, by watching *Beaches* and *My Girl,* and reading *Bridge to Terabithia.* It seemed as if only CC Bloom, Vada Sultenfuss, and Jesse Aarons knew what it was like to lose their best friend and together we shared in our collective sorrow.

Lost without Melissa, Amanda and I grieved separately and unable to face one another we stayed apart for years, cocooned as we were in our own hopelessness.

Eight years old is just too soon to learn how sadness is the most committed of emotions. Unlike happiness, always fleeting or anger, always fading, sadness, once arrived, stays with you and this sadness, like memories of Melissa, has stayed with me since that August day.

The Pooks

But sadness, although solitary, is never sedentary. How it likes to move from place to place, sharing the heaviness of its heart with all those who dare so much as to stand in its way.

They were my cousins and there were four of them: two boys and two girls. John, Ronnie, Kristen, and Michele. All of them, born before us, became our protectors, if only by the default of time, where they alternated between making us laugh and making us cry, dropping us on our heads and picking us up. They lived in Holbrook, in a house on Silva Street. They went to Grundy Elementary School. They went to Seneca Middle School. They went to Sachem High School. For reasons unknown, my brother Nick took to calling them the Pooks and the name stuck.

Their mother was Linda. She was my godmother who wore big thick-rimmed glasses with purple frames and when she wrapped her arms around us, she always smelled and felt as if she had just come out of the dryer on a cold winter's day: warm and soft and clean and fresh. Although the years turned her hair from brown to grey she still wore it cropped just as she had since high school. I remember the way she smiled when she looked at us. I remember the way she smiled when she looked at them. How desperately she loved her children. How desperately she loved us all.

My Uncle John, my mother's brother, their father, was the opposite of his wife: an alcoholic who squeezed too tight and played too rough and whenever he entered a room, I always looked to escape it. Some blame his addiction on the time that he spent in Vietnam, but there must be other ways to forget about war. Although he worked in a furniture store on Jericho Turnpike, he spent more time drinking in the bar next-door than selling kitchenettes and dining room tables. While he worked she stayed home to raise their children even though she was sick and had been sick for longer than she let on.

In 1985, they diagnosed her with cervical cancer. Michele was only seven years old. Kristen was twelve, Ronnie was fourteen, and John was just sixteen; all children who held onto the hope that their mother would get better. But hope is not tangible like a tumor. Sometimes as cancer grows, it is hope that shrinks.

For years my mother drove her for her treatment. Still children, she took us with them whenever they went and we sat in the back of the station wagon playing eye spy with my little eye or the license plate game, but as time went on and her treatment showed little sign of success we sat in silence, watching cars as they passed, some of us living, some of us dying; how cruelly these worlds collide.

This is the way life unravels: in clumps and knots, in pieces and chunks. One day you lose your hair, the next you lose everything else.

In October, they buried her in the same cemetery as Melissa where only the living were left to decide which was worse: a mother to lose her child or children to lose their mother.

There should be a space between deaths; room in which to grieve and mourn and lament a loss before another is lost, but death is one-dimensional, existing only on a single plane, where time collapses, life collapses.

After, life went on, but not in the same way. Never in the same way again.

What it was like without their mother in that house as children as teenagers, I do not know. My memories are pieced together from the scattered nights I slept over, watching scary movies that I was still too young to see: *Nightmare on Elm Street, Halloween,* and *Friday the Thirteenth.* In the morning we sat down to a breakfast of Jell-O Pudding and Pop Tarts. For me, this was a treat, something out of the ordinary. For them it was often the only food they had in the house.

In the last year of the decade:

The Exxon Valdez spilled eleven million gallons of oil into the Prince William Sound.

There was a massacre in Tiananmen Square.

Melissa died.

Aunt Linda died.

The Oakland Athletics won the World Series.

The Berlin Wall fell.

But those are the things that had yet to happen.

It happened at midnight on November 9, 1989, the falling of the Berlin Wall.

In New York it was only 6 o'clock in the evening as we watched the world change before our eyes. On that cold November night I remember being able to see the frozen breath of the citizens from both sides of Berlin as they climbed to the top of the wall; perhaps these were the first full breaths that they had taken in twenty-eight years. In that moment it seemed as if all of Berlin, all of the world, stood on top of that wall crying and embracing, remembering or perhaps learning for the first time what it means to be free. After that night, the Cold War was no more.

How beautiful it was to think, no matter how fleeting of a thought, that we no longer lived in a world where we had to hide underneath our desks in fear of an atomic bomb being dropped, as if elementary schools offered protection from the splitting of atoms and the destruction of the world. Although I was too young to understand the meaning behind words such as Communism or Glasnost or Perestroika, I was old enough to understand that there is a difference between right and wrong, good and evil, war and peace and I was already beginning to understand that if you fight long enough and hard enough repression and oppression can and will be defeated.

I remember, sometime before the falling of the wall, watching Alvin and the Chipmunks, as I did on most Disney Afternoons, but this was the episode that I remember the most. In it, Alvin, Simon, and Theodore were flying with Dave to Germany to put on a concert in West Berlin. Somewhere over the Atlantic Ocean, Alvin fell asleep and dreamt of a world that finally knew peace and in this dream he sang: "*Let the wall come down; tumble to the ground.*" At eight years old, I, too, wanted that wall to fall; afraid that if it were to remain standing, just how many other walls were to be built, how many more wars were to be fought?

That question was answered less than two months later when Operation Desert Storm began in January 1990. From the safety of our living rooms we watched as missiles and other incendiary objects were launched across the Persian Gulf. This was our first introduction to war as spectacle. And yet, on February 11, 1990, Nelson Mandela was released from prison and the Apartheid that separated an entire nation came to an end.

During that winter that straddled a decade, as the world attempted to find balance, I discovered that these historical world events sometimes enveloped and often mirrored my own personal history and were woven into the very fabric of my being; creating a ceaseless pattern of sorrow and wonder, tragedy and triumph, mournings and celebrations, endings and beginnings.

And so began the last year of elementary school.

On the first day of fifth grade, our teacher, Mr. Henner told our entire class that he was born three days before water and that he was older than dirt. Closer to the truth, he was probably in his mid to late forties and his feet stood upon the topsoil of the Cenozoic era and his skin had yet to show the striations left by time. In his class we read George Orwell, we read Sir H. Rider Haggard, and we recited the Preamble to the Declaration of Independence, where we learned that power corrupts and absolute power corrupts absolutely, that adventures are to be had anywhere and everywhere, and none of us are promised happiness, we are only asked to pursue it. And for that year happiness, that innocent happiness, was found learning how to use a computer for the first time, not to surf the world wide web, but to search the world over for Carmen San Diego and to set off on the Oregon Trail hoping that we did not die of dysentery somewhere between Independence, Missouri and Willamette Valley.

But this was a happiness that was not to last…

When he sold the house, they were still living there. They being his four children, all teenagers, without their mother and now without their home. That was when "He", not Uncle John, just him, became a pronoun rather than a proper noun, an abstraction because nothing was concrete anymore. Did he somehow forget they were there? Maybe alcoholism makes you forget you have children. Maybe scotch makes you forget that those children need their father just as much as they need their mother. Maybe cheap beer makes you forget everything and everyone, even yourself.

My mother, long since tired of her brother's detachment from his own children and desperate to provide stability where there was none, asked them to come to live with us. Not all four of them, just Kristen and Michele. Their brothers, boys, almost men, exercised their independence by living elsewhere, further dividing their family that was held together only by the fragility of their loss. That was when the five of us became the seven of us.

For my mother and father the choice was easy. That was what they were supposed to do and since we were still children their choice was ours as well. After all, family is family. The immediacy and the necessity of this decision left it unopened to discussion and the ramifications of which were not carefully considered, among which Newton's Third Law comes to mind. But how were we to know how it would impact all of us?

At first it was exciting because for the first time in my life I had sisters, not cousins because cousins insinuates distance and now there was no distance between them and us. In our house, they shared a room in the basement where they slept on mahogany bunk beds: one of the last remaining vestiges of their home that they were able to bring with them from Holbrook to here. Once in Northport, they taught me how to paint my nails and apply make-up, and do all the things that older sisters are supposed to do with their little sisters, and how I loved them for it.

Kristen, seven years my senior, was the wild one who named her cars Kit, Black Beauty, and Princess. It was in Princess, her 1989 Jeep Cherokee that she introduced us to the Violent Femmes and Rusted Root, playing *Send me on my Way* and *Blister in the Sun* over and over again on her tape deck until we learned every beat, every rhythm, every word. Because she was the oldest among us, and the only one with a license, she became our chauffeur, shuttling us back and forth from practice and school plays, convincing us that she could fit us all in her two door GT (Black Beauty) because there was room in the trunk and we weren't that big just yet. Since she was often the only adult in our house, as our parents went from one job to the next in their effort to keep it all together, she was our chef, our chaperone, and a comedian, stumbling into the basement after a night of debauchery shouting "Rock On" at the top of her lungs and we adored her for it (and still do).

Michele was the youngest in her family and now one of the oldest in ours. She danced and played field hockey and sometimes grew quiet and withdrawn in her attempt to adjust to a new town, a new school, and a new group of friends. She is also an artist and in charcoal, she drew peppers the way that Edward Weston photographed them except our life was anything but still. Most days, Michele thrilled me with stories of her life unchaperoned and I remember envying her freedom without realizing that she would have given it all up just for one more day with her mother.

When the novelty of this new living situation began to fade, I felt how the Western World must have felt when Nicolaus Copernicus and Galileo Galilei proposed that it was not the sun that revolved around the earth, but that it was the earth that revolved around the sun; uncentered and unaware of the fact that gravity is gravity and light is light no matter what your position is among the stars.

On Adolescence

On June 17, 1994, there was a party to celebrate the end of middle school and the beginning of high school where we jumped in and out of the pool acting like the children we so desperately no longer wanted to be. Inside, the television was on; the screen so large that it took up the entire room and for that night and too many nights that followed, it did.

Some time before the cake was brought out and the candles were lit a white Ford Bronco was being 'chased' along the Los Angeles Freeway. In the backseat of the car was O.J. Simpson with a gun to his head and in the driver's seat, Al Cowlings sat with his hands, ungloved, wrapped tightly around the steering wheel.

Somewhere in that long Los Angeles night a woman cries, she has lost her daughter. A father cries, he has lost his son. Children cry, they have lost their mother. A nation cries, they have lost their hero. All across America, all eyes were turned to the west coast and our backs were turned to everywhere else. Somewhere in East Africa, in a nation smaller than the state of California, almost one million Rwandans were being murdered, mutilated, raped, and tortured, and yet, it was only this police chase that made the evening news.

Homicide. Genocide. One death. Two deaths. One million deaths.
Is it all the same?

For an entire year the media spectacle that was the O.J. Simpson trial played on every television screen and adorned the front pages of every newspaper across the country. In the commons of the high school boys in their football jerseys stood in front of the screen mesmerized by the pageant. How they celebrated when he was acquitted, how they whooped and cheered and gave each other high fives as if this verdict of not guilty was no different than a Tiger home team victory on a Saturday afternoon.

It was not until over ten years later, one cold February night, that I learned the extent of the horrors of that June night and the hundred surrounding nights of the Rwandan genocide, when I watched *Sometimes in April*. Afterwards, I wept. I wept for Tutsis. I wept for Hutus. I wept for Rwanda. I wept for the world.

High school had begun…

High school: the place where is learned the cruelties of the world. Here, there is no god of fairness. There is no patron saint of the golden rule. Here, there are no rules. So, like most teenage girls, I acted out the theatrical and overly dramatic phases of my adolescence by projecting my insecurities upon the world. Some days I cast myself in the role of the mean girl, the bitch, and the bully, and other days I would have chosen sticks and stones and broken bones rather than the names that always hurt me for those were the days when the hallway was the most terrible place to walk.

If ever there was an awkward time in my life, between the ages of fourteen and eighteen was it. I arrived in high school less than five feet tall, less that one hundred pounds, with teeth that were less than straight. For me, puberty was only a rumor, periods were still what was attached to the ends of sentences, and, try as I might, Victoria never did tell me her secret. To have to go through puberty when you are in middle school or high school is a punishment worse than death. It is bad enough that you are forced to share a school, a grade, and a class with your sworn enemy, but to do so while you are at your most vulnerable, your least confident, your most maladroit is just plain awful.

Thanks to Judy Bloom I spent hours squeezing my elbows together whispering: *"I must, I must, I must increase my bust."* Always underdeveloped, my mother told me that in her sixteenth year, she woke up with a full C cup. Her tits practically grew overnight. So from the moment I turned sixteen, and for almost an entire year after, as soon as I opened my eyes, I looked down hoping to find mountains where only molehills abound, but my chest stayed flat. Not even my feet, of which I had an unadulterated view, grew.

Judy Bloom and my mother be damned.

There are things that happen in a day that are within our control; like the last ski run down the mountain before the chairlifts close; my friend Dana and I racing one another and the soon to be setting sun, poles tucked, knees bent, forever in competition with the wind. And then there are things that happen in a day that are beyond our control: A car accident. A roof collapsed. And a life that spirals out of control.

That winter, the roof of my father's factory, laden with snow, caved in, destroying decades of my father's hard work. Still believing himself to be invincible, even after all these years, he kept no insurance on this building. Nothing was to be recovered. Everything had been lost.

To compensate for these irreparable losses my mother took one job and then another, determined as she was that no other roofs were to be lost over our heads. But it was not only the roof that collapsed that February, our whole world collapsed with it, and all that was left was us: My father without a job, my cousins without their mother, my mother without her sanity; five teenagers and only two parents when there used to be four. When the money that had been taken for granted for too many years slowly disappeared chaos became our commodity, which was traded in bulk, but never bargained for.

In the months that followed my family lived in denial, so much so that when my parents won a trip to London in the spring of my sophomore year they attempted to salvage what was left of our familial wreckage and took us with them to the United Kingdom, even though they could little afford this extravagance. Needless to say, economics was never among the many lessons that I have learned from my parents. It might have also been that they were unwilling to leave their teenage children behind, all alone, in their house for ten days while they travelled across the pond or it might have been their simple desire to show us the world. Either way, all we went, begrudgingly and reluctantly on this family vacation; a vacation which not only sparked the flames for all of my travels to come, it also ignited another inextinguishable fire among another member of our family.

In England, an apartment was rented close to Hyde Park and we did all the things that must be done when in London for the first time. In one afternoon we sipped High Tea at Harrods's, we ate dinner at Simpson's, and we saw Miss Saigon in the West End. All other afternoons we sought out history wherever it was to be found. At the Tower of London we listened to tales of executions and imprisonments and in Westminster Abbey we walked among kings and poets. We wandered and wondered around Stonehenge, dragging our fingers across the monolithic rocks weathered by time and the curiosity of touch. At Buckingham Palace we witnessed the changing of the guard. We saw the Queen. And we almost started a revolution of our own when the Fourth of July came and went without so much as a hot dog, a s'more, or even a firework.

The only bomb bursting in air exploded on our last night in London, when my brother Nick, no more than seventeen, disappeared. My parents worried and fretted and paced the floors of our foreign flat and searched the streets for their son, but he was nowhere to be found. When he returned 'home' well past midnight there was no remorse and he offered neither apology nor explanation for where he had been. My brother simply did not care. Had my parents known that this was just the beginning? That somehow his indifference regarding his own life heralded his indifference for the rest of us? Perhaps his was the initial reaction along a chain not to be

65

broken until thermodynamic non-equilibrium was reached.

On Brothers:
Adopted or Otherwise

My relationship with my brother Nick has always been one of tumult and turbulence. Maybe it began when I locked him in a suitcase when I was four and he was six, or maybe it was after. But from that night on I do not remember a time in which my tolerance for Nick stretched longer than an hour at a time. Perhaps, without knowing it, I had sensed his pain and his despair and unable to alleviate his anguish, I only exacerbated it. Had I known that he was to spend his whole life in a prison of his own making I might not have followed the zigzag of the zipper along all three of its edges. But then, as now, I was only concerned with my own freedom.

With him in them rooms became smaller, my heart became smaller. For spite, I hated everything that Nick loved: Seinfeld, ketchup on my eggs, and Zelda. And I loved everything that he hated: Elton John, tomatoes, and the world beyond my own walls.

In elementary school he took an I.Q. test on which he scored higher than most. This test indicated that not only is my brother smart, he might even be considered a genius. Afterward, he was placed in the gifted and talented program, but I am not certain if my brother ever believed that he was gifted or talented. If he ever forgave himself for being smart, I do not know. To be cool, to be popular, to be accepted; these are the things that he longed for the most. For him, his brilliance was a burden, one that he never seemed able to carry and, rather than embrace what made him different, he allowed it to swallow him- whole. Maybe this is why people should learn of all the ways that they are similar before they learn of the ways in which they were different because differences, once recognized, more often separate rather than unite.

In the spring of 1996, Nick was accepted into the Honor's Program at a state university. Whereas my brother may have found success in whichever endeavor he chose, college granted him too much freedom and Nick made the most of this newfound freedom when he discovered drugs. As always, it began with pot and the occasional experimentation with mushrooms. But it did not stop there. It being the late nineties, ecstasy became his drug of choice. Ecstasy- what a strange name for the hell it creates. But then again, what better way to quiet your demons than to pretend that they do not exist?

Was this when his addiction began? It is hard to say for sometimes it is difficult to tell when the light fades from the day and the darkness of night begins. All that is known is that from those early days my brother had fallen into the darkest and deepest of oubliettes from which there was no escape and from then on, he was Icarus, both with and without wings.

When he failed out of college his first semester he came home with diamond studs in his ears and his hair bleached blonde. On the nights that my parents were not home, their kitchen became a chemistry lab. But my brother was neither an alchemist nor was he attempting to complete what Mendeleev began. Instead, he tried to create a counterfeit version of what he sold, for by then, my brother was not only doing drugs, he was selling them too. After he was satisfied with this chemistry experiment, he disappeared for days on end. No one knew where he was and it was only my mother and father who cared. Neither Chris nor Kristen nor Michele nor I gave a fuck where it was that he went for without him there our house was almost quiet and our lives were almost normal, but even when he was not here and I tried to speak to my parents about what their son was doing it was like warning them of wolves as my brother huffed and puffed and blew our house down.

During that time it was always hard to tell what was more difficult for my parents: when he was gone or when he came back.

If and when he finally returned, he was strung out and the chemical cocktail that he had ingested over the course of the weekend had begun to withdraw from his body. Coming down, he slept in the room that he still shared with Chris with the shades down, the lights off, and the darkness all-encompassing. This was no longer a cry for help- it was a scream, a wail, a howl bellowing into the night and during the day, just a whimper. In black light paint he wrote the lyrics of *Release* on the ceiling, almost invisible in the shining of the sun and glowing soft and purple in the twilight. In his idle hours did he lay on his back on the top bunk asking for the very same thing?

Unable to understand the ways in which his pain mirrored my own I fought him using all of the bad words that could be mustered from my ever expanding vocabulary of profanity, but when words failed to inflict the damage I so desired and rage turned violent we went to blows even though I knew I was the underdog in this fight. That was when he dragged me by my hair across the backyard punching and kicking me in the dirt and grass. I tried to fight back, but there is only so much strength contained within the body of a prepubescent teenage girl who weighed less than one hundred pounds. And besides, it only made things worse. And still, I kept fighting on.

For some reason it was never enough for him to put holes in his brain, he had to inflict pain on those in his immediate vicinity. Whatever pains my brother was going through, he was determined to share it with our entire family. As if pain was transferrable. But pain does not work like that. Pain cannot be shared. Pain can only be experienced on our own and the only drug that can take this pain away, that can strip it of its strength, its power, its force, is time.

For years I hated him. I hated him for having to include all of us in his torture. I hated him for his weakness. I hated him for throwing away his life for more lows than highs. I hated what he did to himself and what he did to the rest of us and this hate consumed my entire being, devouring all else for when you are young and have not yet learnt just how imperfect us frail humans can be there is no room for patience, there is no room for compassion, and there most certainly is no such thing as empathy. There is only hatred. Pure hatred. And anger; boy was there anger. And this anger, the most radioactive and reactive of human emotions, was violent and unstable. (But, anger, too, has its half-life).

I do not know what these years were like for him, I neither asked nor cared, but for us, for me, witnessing his descent was like discovering the existence of black holes once and for all. Stand too close and you might just get pulled in. Stand too far and you might continue to doubt their existence, their violence, and their gravitas.

Addiction, pain, fear, darkness without light; these are the things of which dark matter is made.

How Nick's drug addiction affected the rest of my family is difficult to say, but it was not only he who lashed out on our new set of circumstances. I, too, found ways to rebel and revolt, for when your years are few and your emotions are many you learn just how difficult it is to abide by the laws of unintended consequences.

Thereafter, our house, long the scene of scuffles and skirmishes, became a full-blown war zone with battles being fought and nothing being won. These were the years that gave the words nuclear family a whole new meaning. How we made it through I do not know. Perhaps my family is made of elastic; we stretch without severing, we bend without breaking. We keep going. No. Matter. What.

But when things were at their worst, when my mother was at her worst, when I was at my worst- it took me up until now to stop blaming her for this entropic life, as if somehow it was her fault that the second law of thermodynamics exists in the first place- we fought the battles which most teenagers wage against their mothers, her trying she to fight for my love and me denying her of that complicated pleasure. In our house there was never a day without an explosion, rarely a day without a fight.

Like an animal torn from the wild and placed in captivity, I growled and scowled and paced the cage of my own making just waiting for some reason, any reason to pounce on my mother and when the opportunity presented itself, as was inevitable, only venom escaped my lips: *I hate you. I hate you. I hate you. I hate you.*

Unable to see beyond my own rage, I kicked and I screamed, I punched and I yelled. I was a banshee, a keening woman, weeping and wailing my lamentations upon the world. Sometimes she pushed back, but most of the time my mother not so patiently waited it out, as she has for almost every tantrum I have thrown since birth, for we are not oil and vinegar. We are fire and fire. We are one and the same.

But just when she thought I had finished, when all the rage seemed to have subsided, she asked the question she has always asked at the end of each and every one of my tirades: *"Briana, why are you doing this?"* I do not say, *"I don't know."* I do not tell her it is because I am scared or that I am afraid or that I am unable to control myself. No. I am too proud and too stubborn for confessions such as these. Instead, I tell her that I hate her again and again and that I want nothing more than for her to leave me the fuck alone, that I did not need anyone, especially not her, and that I wished that she was not my mother and that this was not my family.

Sometimes, after there was no more fight left in either of us, I heard her sobs unmuffled through the wall that separated her bedroom from mine. Was I the daughter she so desperately wanted? Was I the child she prayed for? Perhaps now she prayed that she could take it all back, but there is no return policy for prayers once they are answered.

On the days that my mother came home from one job only to leave for another, she would cry, shout and scream at one of us, or all of us all at once. Frustrated, overwhelmed, but never defeated, she told my father that she wanted a divorce, that she no longer wanted the love and the life that she had created and that she wanted out from the life that only she was strong enough to lead. In these instances she was like the boy who cried wolf; never meaning it, but we all feared it just the same.

My father, never one for many words, did not fight back. How little I understood or accepted his passivity, often mistaking it for cowardice, but my father was no more of a coward than my mother was a beast.

One day, when all hell was loose and life seemed to be falling apart at the seams, my mother sped away, threatening to never come back. I, being the insubordinate, irreverent teenager that I was, tried to convince my father that maybe that wasn't such a bad thing and that divorce wasn't such a bad idea either, as if those seven letters were the answer to every single one of their problems. And yet, he answered me with seven words that forever changed my life, seven words that have yet to be forgotten:

"You have no idea what love is."

My father was right: of love I knew nothing.

And still, for most of that decade and the decade that followed I continued to shun their unconditional love, convincing myself that I did not need anyone or anything and that alone was where I was supposed to be. I was a teenager fighting with the world. It was a war that lasted many angst filled years; years trying to make sense of a world about which, I also knew nothing.

On Being an Athlete

With so many things happening at once: a full house, an unemployed father, an overworked mother, a drug addicted brother, and teenagers who did not know which end was up, I needed an departure, however temporarily, into a world separate from my family and entirely my own. So as to escape, I turned to sports, that beautiful arena in which all that can comfortably and uncomfortably be learned about the world and ourselves takes place. It began with soccer and basketball, and then, come high school, field hockey and lacrosse. Perhaps my brother Chris did the same. Perhaps all of those hours and all of those years spent outside catching and throwing and passing manifested into an athletic addiction where routine and repetition balanced the contrariness of our home.

What I loved the most about lacrosse was that there were no boundaries, except for fences that sometimes, but not always, surrounded the field. Then, there were no out of bounds; there was only one line that, as a midfielder, could not be crossed. Here, on open fields under open skies was ushered the seasons as they passed: the last remnants of summer, the first signs of spring, the slow decay of autumn, and the harsh winds of winter. All of these seasons brought with them a peace unfound anywhere else except here and that peace was more profound than any victory conceded or defeat suffered on that field.

When I was fifteen I was lucky enough to have one of the best coaches of my life who let us play the game as it was meant to be played: fast and ferocious, wild and free. I do not remember how many games we won that year, nor do I remember how many games we lost. I only remember falling so completely in love with this game that it also completed me. A stick, a ball, and a pair of cleats: sometimes these are the only things we need to make us whole.

At the end of my sophomore year, still less than five feet tall, I was brought up to varsity even though there was still so much of the game that needed to be learned. But there I was with two new coaches, both body builders who had retired from the industry in order to coach high school girls lacrosse. One was a gentle giant, but his wife was a beast of a woman, born on a Tuesday, who is still the most intimidating person that I have ever met. Her love was tough if it was even love at all. Under their watchful eyes we practiced on the wall, off the wall, with sticks, without sticks, on defense, on offense, until we got it right, which did not always happen, but hey, that is why it is called practice.

When season began in the spring of my senior year, I did not start even though I had already committed to play at the collegiate level. Between being a four-year starter for the field hockey team and barely seeing the field in lacrosse- aside from the unadulterated view of the field from the bench on the days we had games- where had I gone wrong? But then again, my love for sports, all sports, was so great that I was willing to sit on the sidelines rather than give them up. For me, quitting was never an option. I needed lacrosse because I needed the freedom of the field. But still, it was enough to make one wonder: Was I not an athlete after all?

At seventeen I was unable to understand how coaches were able to treat children in the manner that they do and still call themselves coaches at all. At worst, a coach stifles the spirit, exercising a control in the lives of others that often cannot be found in their own. At best, a coach miraculously points out your wings and reminds you of your ability to fly. More often than not coaches are a little bit of both.

It was because of this, even after the longest of practices, which included the fastest of sprints, the endless laps, the countless suicides that I found the road; the only place where I never lost and where I was the only one who got to decide where I started and where I ended. The road never told me that I was not good enough, big enough, or fast enough. And this road absorbed all of my pain, all of my anger, all of my fear, and all of my frustration, never asking for anything in return. And this road was where I went when it seemed as if there was nowhere else to go.

There were days when the rains began to fall sometime after the first mile, soft at first and then coming down sideways or from the ground up. But I did not turn around, I did not seek shelter from this storm. Determined never to hide when faced with adversity I kept going, step after step, mile after mile. When the rain showed no signs of stopping, neither did I, and, finally surrendering, I ran down the hill with my arms open and my eyes closed, and in that moment, I was free.

Somewhere in the middle of this Stella got sick. Almost every night after lacrosse practice we drove to the hospital; my father behind the wheel and the three of us staring silently out the windows onto roads that we now knew by heart. By the time we arrived in the corridor where she was intubated, the late spring sky was enveloped in darkness and the chill of what still remained of winter returned to the air. She was in the hospital because her diabetes had caused failures in her heart. Shortly thereafter, she had a stroke surviving just long enough for us to say goodbye.

Not only did my father lose his business that year, he lost his mother, and maybe he also lost his faith that life, once fair, would always be fair. But life does not fight fair; it never did, it never will.

On a Saturday in May we buried my grandmother. Here again was death. It was not that I needed or wanted to believe my family to be immortal, it was that these lessons in mortality caused me to question all other beliefs regarding love and life and made me wonder just how unnecessary it might be to believe in anything at all.

That night, so as to forget, I drank tequila and then beer and then tequila again so much and so fast that the room spun and it only stopped long enough for me to meet my first love, after which, the room began to spin again and with an embarrassment that I am still mortified of to this day, I tossed my cookies right there in front of him, which must have made quite the impression because he called me the next day to see about a baseball game and he called me everyday that summer after that.

He was home from college between his freshman and sophomore year. He was tall, handsome, smart, athletic and ambitious: everything I wanted, but could not accept. Rather than finding comfort in the love that he offered I raged against it, clinging too tightly to pain and heartbreak, as if those were my only possibilities in this life. And still, despite my most adamant protestations, I became his girlfriend and he became my boyfriend. We kissed, we watched fireworks and maybe, just maybe, I began to learn what love is. But September came and that old fear returned when he went back to Boston to begin his second year of college. So great was this fear of worthiness that to spite my face I cut off my nose and took back my heart just to convince myself that I did not need anyone, not even him.

Perhaps it was ideas of senior year that crept into my heart or perhaps it was the freedom that I had just been granted in not only getting a license, but in having a car that caused me to make so callous a decision. But this license and this car granted me the very things I so craved: to be alone and to be free. Two things that I then believed ceased to exist when you share your heart with another.

And yet, it was never the great distances that I travelled to in this car, it was those places closer and nearer to my heart that I returned in order to remember and to never forget. Without leaving the limits of Northport I found myself underneath the Japanese Maple that was planted to commemorate Melissa's death. There, a stone lays upon the grass with her name etched into the granite and a seagull with wings spread wide soars over a ripple of waves below. At all times of day, but mostly at night, I sat under the branches of this tree wondering how different life would have been if Melissa were still alive. Would she help me to understand all of the things that could not be understood? Would she share in this confusion? Or would she simply say to hell with everything?

Some people refer to their high school years as glory days or the best days of their life but give me now, give me today, give me tomorrow, give me ambiguity, and give me uncertainty but please, please, please, please do not ever give me high school again.

On College

The final decision in choosing a college came down to two uncontestable factors: whether they had a women's lacrosse team and whether they offered a program in international affairs. To be fair, if I could not be a diplomat in my own home, however could I expect to be a diplomat anywhere else? Originally, I had wanted to go to Gettysburg College, haunted as it is by ghosts of the Civil War, but Fredericksburg, too, has its history. In this small southern town the Rappahannock River winds its way north from the Chester Gap to the Chesapeake Bay. During the Revolutionary War, George Washington stationed his mother, Mary, here. It was just close enough to keep her safe and just far enough away so she was not able to meddle in affairs of the state. Many years after, a Civil War battle was fought along the riverbank, a battle in which the rebels won, so perhaps I being the rebel that believed myself to be and our home host to its own civil war of sorts, going to college was my secession from my familial union.

My mother fell in love with Fredericksburg well before I did. Maybe it reminded her of Northport with its hills and its main street and its small town charm. Maybe, like George Washington, the distance was just far enough away for her, but for me, it was never far enough. So when that August came I happily packed my bags and headed to Mary Washington College to play lacrosse and to study all kinds of history. In these bags came all of my anger and all of my resentment, all of my rage and all of my Northern aggression. Who says you can't take it with you?

But it is only now that I realize that this anger was only sadness metastasized by things incomprehensible for a girl who had not experienced enough of life to understand just how applicable the laws of physics are to the human experience.

And so it was with this anger I left Long Island and entered the South, which was so very different than the world that I left behind and it was here that I was lucky enough to encounter friends who have remained my friends in all of the years since- and hopefully, all the years to come. For sometimes a moment is all that it takes for a friendship to form and last a lifetime.

College began with Lauren: my roommate freshman year. She, too, was from New York, but she was full of the softness of Westchester County and none of the harshness of Long Island. Our friendship was formed bonding over all of the things that white girls in college bond about: Dave Matthews Band and cute boys, cute boys and the Dave Matthews Band. We were assigned to live in a triple with a girl from Virginia whose love of Coca-Cola was only surpassed by her love to stay in bed. All. Damn. Day. Every. Damn. Day. Our room was only a fraction larger than the room that I had left behind, except that this room was crowded with a bunk bed and a twin bed, three dressers, three desks and three young women who learned all too quickly the effects of confined spaces on adolescent girls. It was a difficult year, one in which we fought and did our best not to kill one another. Had it not been for Lauren, the keeper of sanity, I might have finally gone off the deep end once and for all.

And then there was Ryan. He, too, was from Northport and was two years older than us. From the moment I arrived at Mary Washington, this ever-protective watch fellow took both Lauren and I under his forever expanding wings. For the two years we spent together in college he watched out for us and made sure that we all got home safe after the parties he threw at his house off campus. In Ryan I found not only the older brother that I had always wanted, but also the one that I had always needed.

And there was Jesse; the most love-driven, passionate man that I have ever been blessed enough to call my friend. How quickly he became (and remains) my favorite person in the whole wide world. In quiet places, we shared the secrets and stories of our souls. And we laughed, mostly about nothing but the sheer pleasure of being alive.

It is with regret that the mention of these boys is ever so brief, not only because of the lasting effect that they have had on my life, but also because throughout college and after, Jesse and Ryan were my rocks, more so my boulders and my shoulders to stand on, to lean on, and to playfully punch from time to time. And what they should have been was the standard that I held myself to when it came to dating all other men. But then again, all of my 'mistakes' would have been less fun if that were the case.

In an English class, I met Katie. She was also New Yorker, but so very different than the jocks with which I spent most of my time, so naturally I gravitated towards her. Shortly after we became friends she introduced me to the man who I have been in love with ever since: Tom Robbins. When she handed me her battered copy of *Another Roadside Attraction,* its jacket cover torn and the pages dog-eared and crisp from being once wet and now dry, she told me that this was the book that I had to read and forsake all others. And so began a love affair that has lasted for decades; one that has taken me to the jungles of South America, the streets of Paris, the pyramids at Giza, and a ranch out west, if only to feast on Tibetan Peach Pie. It was a love affair that taught me more about religion, government, philosophy, sexuality, and sensuality than any of the classes that were taken at Mary Washington College.

And finally, there are two words that I learned in college that, when recalled, return me, over and over again, to what it is like to be young, to be wild, and to be free. Those words are Amber Byer.

Back when drinking was a sport and hangovers were things of myths and legends, a party was held at Ryan's house on High Street. As usual, it was crowded and full of college kids doing what college kids do best: shotgunning beers, shouting for absolutely no reason, and demonstrating just how desperately they needed to practice the art of kissing. To escape the debauchery of which we were always more than willing participants, we went across the street to the baseball field and sat on the otherwise empty bleachers. I do not remember how much we had been drinking and for all I know, we could have been sober, but that night we watched a baseball game that only she and I could see and so we cheered on an invisible team in the darkness:

Hey batta, batta, batta

What do you say 2-2?

Come on now…

That night, we were the queens of wishful drinking and in that moment we became the bestest of friends for everyone in the world needs a friend like Amber. A friend that does not need to convince you that playing forty-five cup beer pong on a Monday afternoon is a good idea even though you have an exam the next day that you have not even begun to study for, a friend who still chooses to be on your team for turbos long after you have given up

90

drinking for lacrosse season, and a friend that can come into your room without knocking and crawl into bed with you without the need to say a single word. And a friend who reminds you, every so gently, but ever so honestly, after every heartbreak, after every disappointment, and after the days that never go according to plan, of this and only this:

Never sell yourself short because all of the fun rides require you to be tall.

Maybe it was because of our shenanigans together that when the grades came in for the first semester I skated by with a 1.25. Although it was not quite failing, it was pretty darn close. But hey, it's not everyday that one's body weight and one's GPA are one and the same. Perhaps my academic aspirations, like my GPA, should have been quite a bit higher.

That winter break I wanted to quit college and run off to Paris. Let's be honest: everyday running off to Paris is always the first option no matter what the surrounding circumstances, but then again I also knew that not only did I need an education, I wanted one as well. So maybe it was that at that time I was a little lost and a little distracted. Maybe it was that I was a *femme perdue.*

In January, I returned to college for no other reasons than to continue to learn and because lacrosse season was about to begin and, as with high school, it was only on the field, the battlefield, where I was not lost, I was found. As a freshman I started every single game, scoring a goal or two along the way. By the end of the season, we were ranked in the top ten in the nation and I had more than doubled my GPA that second semester; hardly a *fait accompli,* but it was a start.

College went on. Freshman year ended and sophomore year began.

If ever you longed to witness magic mention one word to anyone who calls this Island home: Summer. Then, you will see eyes that light up in both remembrance of days past and anticipation of days to come. These memories, like the heat that rises in June and lasts well into September, warm even the coldest of winter days and it is sometimes only summer that makes those that live on Long Island stay on Long Island. But that summer was different than all other summers, at least for us and most especially for Nick.

One July afternoon the party stopped for Nick, for that was the day when the cops arrived with their search warrants and their handcuffs and their flashing lights and flashing badges. They came to arrest him for selling ecstasy to an undercover cop; too much to be considered a misdemeanor and just the right amount to be considered a felony.

But that day it was not Nick who exercised his right to remain silent. It was us. I watched from my window as they put him in the backseat of their patrol car, the lights strobing red and blue, and I continued to stare long after they drove away with my brother hunched down in the back failing in his attempt to hide the tears in his eyes. Nick, who could have gone anywhere and done anything, was going to jail. In my *schadenfreude* I was glad to see him go, happy that he had finally been caught, and hoping that maybe this would put and end to his addiction once and for all, or, at the very least, an end to our torment. If only life were that simple.

His arrest devastated my mother and father. Of course they knew that this day might come, but still they feared it nonetheless. But for me, by then, the hate in my heart had grown so dark that it eclipsed any compassion that I might have had for him, and not only did I celebrate his imminent incarceration, I found a smug amount of satisfaction in the fact that we did not share the same blood. Was I so cold and heartless or was the pain that I was experiencing so great that I tried and failed and tried again to convince myself that I did not care just to lessen the hurt that was my heart? Either way, my absence of empathy in this moment did little to allay the pain that persisted for all of the years to follow.

That this familial tragedy was part of the greater unease of the world made it all the more tragic. At the end of the millennia, the whole world lived in a perpetual state of fear and apocalyptic uncertainty. There was a mass shooting at Columbine High School (the first in my lifetime), genocide in Bosnia-Serbia (the second in my lifetime), ethnic conflict the world over, and the ever-present AIDS epidemic that had now, at the end of the century, claimed the lives of 18.8 million people. And yet, on New Years Eve, December 31, 1999, Y2K, when everything was supposed to come crashing down around us, the world did not end, it simply kept spinning, unaware and unconcerned of our own human futility.

I returned to college to begin my junior year. This was a time to move off campus and start practicing 'adulthood.' At 800 Wolfe Street, there were six of us living under one roof. We were all lacrosse players except one. How anyone thought that this was a good idea is beyond me, but there we were, six young girls pretending to be grown-ups when we so obviously were not.

Perhaps it was because my mother had read to me from *The Little Princess* too many times as a child that I chose the attic, a room with no insulation; only plywood and shingles, plastic sheathing for walls, and wooden slats that did not extend to the roofline. I chose this room for no other reason but its isolation, reasoning that if I removed myself from the world I might finally find peace. But this peace was not yet possible because I still found contentment in the wars that I waged upon any and all possible happiness that entered my life. And still I loved that room except in the dead of winter when the space heater did little to stave off the coldness that crept through the thin walls or the height of summer when one learns all too quickly just how determined heat is to rise.

Sequestered from the rest of the house, I read books without distraction, underlining words and lines that echoed the song in my heart. After, I listened to Joni Mitchell's *Miles of Aisles* on my Fischer-Price record player for hours, flipping the vinyl from side A to side B, as if it was the only record in the world. Sometimes I imagined myself with a guitar instead of a lacrosse stick because at twenty, I still operated under the belief that in this life you can only be one thing at a time instead of everything all at once. Perhaps that is why, when it came to choosing majors, I chose to study the history of art instead of international affairs because that is exactly what art is: EVERYTHING. ALL. AT. ONCE. Besides, the history of art offered a stillness and a silence that was not found anywhere else in my life.

It began with ARTH 101 and has yet to cease. In the sacred spaces of Melchers Hall the click of the slide projector pierced through the darkness relaying upon the wall the story of man from the beginning of time. Here we witnessed his wars, his peace, his cities, his pastures, his defeats, his victories, his ugliness, and his beauty. And these stories were told on the ceiling of the Sistine Chapel, in the valleys of kings long forgotten, and on the streets the world over.

In the spring we studied American landscape painting with a

professor who read to us from *Leaves of Grass* and *Les Fleurs du Mal.* Over the course of that semester were mesmerized by the artists of the Hudson River School and their quest for the sublime. One day, just as class was about to begin, our professor had us move our desks to the edges of the room and gathered us in front of a painting by Albert Bierstadt and as the track lighting illuminated the artist's rendition of the *Valley of the Yosemite* he cued John Denver's *Rocky Mountain High.* And in that moment we knew that this was art, this was history, and this was our professor. The very same man who told us:

I like contemporary art. I like Matthew Barney. I like videos of men sowing up their scrotum. I like Jeff Koon's' Michael Jackson and Bubbles. I like Kiki Smith's bottles of bodily fluids. I like it because it is completely rebellious and appeals to my rebellious nature.

And why not? Art is rebellion after all and had it not been for art the constant rebellion that swelled up inside of me life would have taken a more cynical and more contemptuous turn, a turn only towards darkness and never towards light.

For my twentieth birthday we had a "bring your own bottle" party at Wolfe Street, but it was not vodka in plastic bottles or bottom of the barrel whiskey that proved to be the best gift of the night. Instead, it was a small paperback book, little more than three hundred pages. On its cover was a boy of eleven, riding a broomstick. His wire-rimmed glasses were held together with tape and on his forehead was a scar in the shape of a lightening bolt. His name was Harry Potter and for the first time since high school I fell in love with a boy: The Boy Who Lived.

And so began another of the greatest love affairs of my life; one that brought as much joy and sorrow into my life as anything in my world of reality. For this book, above all others, proved that we are all conjurers of our own spells, we are all wielders of wands, and we are all capable of magic and miracles. Once picked up, it was impossible to put down and I spent what time that was not consumed with lacrosse and school, consuming the pages of this book and all other books in the series that followed. I read in my room, in the hallways, but most of all, I read out of doors in a place where no one could find me, a place quite the opposite of the cupboard under the stairs.

When the leaves lost their summer luster and began to burn their fading hues of red and golden and Orion, the eternal hunter, was revealed in the autumn sky, I went down to the river even though it was salt water for which my soul ached. At the top of an outcropping of limestone and sandstone that rose above the Rappahannock, I went to read and write and listen to the rush of the water as it flowed between rocks and under the low lying limbs that caressed the ever moving river with its branches. Although this river traverses almost two hundred miles from the place where it springs forth from the wind gap of the Blue Mountains to where it empties into Chesapeake Bay, it was in this place where it seemed as if it were without beginning and without end. And it was to this place that I came to revel in the untamed earth, the rains when they fell, and a history long since past.

On December 11, 1862 a battle was fought between two armies of a once same nation, in which the Confederacy won. There are tales that are told about how at night, after the fighting for the day had ended, the soldiers from the North and the South would wade across the river to trade what little goods they had and share stories of both war and an ever evasive peace. Perhaps it was also here that they celebrated an early Christmas. I would like to think that in these moments of shared camaraderie that the war that they were fighting against one another was almost forgotten, if only for those cold nights that passed all too swiftly before the rising of the sun ascended over their encampments, bringing darkness rather than light once more.

I stayed there on this hill until the sun fell below the trees and night cast its shadows across the river. Perhaps I, too, was searching for peace long lost along these banks. But this peace I could not find for sometimes the battle without does not and cannot compare to the battle within and mine, no matter how far away from the front lines that I may have fled, was a battle that raged and raged and raged, and, like this river, was without beginning and without end.

Thoughts on Suicide

There were nights, too many nights, when sleep did not come and the world grew louder rather than softer. Outside, rain fell on the roof and the wind crept under the eaves, rattling the windowpanes as cars passed on the street. On the floors below, doors opened and closed as roommates came and went in the night. As one day turned into another I could not sleep, kept awake by the notion that there was always to be too many questions and not enough answers. These were the nights where my thoughts were so heavy that their weight of their chains crushed both my head and my heart. At that time, I had not yet grown comfortable with the haphazard ways in which my mind worked. So fearful was I of the thoughts that entered my head that I all too willingly became their midnight prisoner. When I tried my hardest not to think at all it quickly proved to be a feat impossible, for this was sadness inescapable.

During these bouts of brooding and morbid rumination I tossed and turned in the middle of my bed, begging for sleep to come, but it never did. After years of living in not so silent rage, I had grown tired of fighting a war without mercy or compassion against everything that I could not and perhaps would never understand. I was tired of fighting with my mother, my father, my brothers, my friends, and my coach. Most of all, I was tired of fighting my nemesism, for there were days, too many days, where I even boxed with my own shadow for the darkness.

Sometimes, after midnight, a train passed, an iron horse in the distance. It came from afar, sounding its steam trumpet, alerting the world of its presence. Still awake I listened as it approached, a welcome distraction from my own disquietude.

On the nights when tears filled my eyes more than hope filled my heart I longed to go down to the tracks that ran parallel to my house if only to step over the rails and onto the ties and ballast and stand in the path of the train and watch the headlamp grow brighter and brighter and listen as the engine grow louder and louder until all was quiet once again. A most violent end. But to those tracks I never went. In my room I stayed until the wind no longer howled and the rain fell no more.

Tonight was not the night to learn what few things there are more powerful than a locomotive.

Tonight was only the night to learn that depression and sadness are not to become our enemies. We must be forgiving of our grief and our sorrow; they know not their burden.

On Lacrosse

Forever fearful of falling into the abyss from which there is no escape, I escaped to the lacrosse field. It was here and only here, on the battleground, where I was able to learn the difference between fighting against and fighting for.

At night, long after practice was over, when the field was lit only from streetlights and the headlights of passing cars, I went there by myself, jumping over the fence and kicking off my flip-flops to feel the cool wet grass under my feet. Up and down the field I ran, barefoot, yearning forever to remain in this world without boundaries, the only place, aside from the sea, where I was free.

Perhaps sensing my strife in this angst filled adolescence, our goalie's mother encouraged me during games to sing a song, any song, in order to reign in all that was wild inside of me. It did not have to be out loud, but loud enough for all else to grow quiet. For this, only Nina Simone's *Feeling Good* would do. Lining up on the circle before the game began, I sang this song. How many times it was sung, I do not know. But I sang and I sang and I sang and I played and I played and I played and, more often than not, we won and we won and we won.

And yet surprisingly despite the independence I so longed for from my family, I sought the opposite on the field. There are those who say that you should only be able to count your friends on one hand, but I cannot help but disagree. In my life as an athlete I have been able to count so many more than that both on and off the field. One pass. One catch. One goal. One assist is all it takes to solidify a friendship, to forge a teammate. Year in and year out these girls were my sisters, my family, and my tribe. And in this tribe we won as a team, we lost as a team, we defended one another, we went on the attack together, and we stood by each other's sides because that is just what teammates do.

This is not to say that because I was part of a team that my rage subsided. Quite the contrary, it only fueled the flames. As with most of the adults that I encountered in my adolescence, I had a tumultuous relationship with my college lacrosse coach. Maybe it was me. Maybe it was her. Maybe it was the both of us battling our demons and pitting them one against the other. After practice, when the rest of the team had left the field, she pulled me aside to speak with me, to yell at me, or simply try to tame me unable to realize just how impossible of a task that is.

The optimist in me had hoped that maybe she knew how much I needed to be pushed or maybe she knew how great of a distraction lacrosse was for me and that perhaps, if I focused all of my energy on sport, there would be little energy left for anything else. But then again, the pessimist in me recalls all of the times when she told me that I marched to the beat of my own drum; as if nonconformity was something to be punished, rather than fostered. It was not difficult to tell that she meant this more as a criticism than a compliment, so I simply responded:

"Darn it, Dana, it cannot not be helped. Even after all these years, I am still dancing to the Rhythm of the Saints."

It was only after leaving the field that I made a promise to myself, which has has remained unbroken all of these years later. I promised to never ever ever let my fire go out, to never let my flames subside or be extinguished, but to always be that spark that blazes and burns, forever shining a light into the darkness. These promises were made as well:

To never surrender.
To refuse to quit.
To believe in the impossible.
To Listen to my heart.
And to always live my dreams. Always.

And these dreams came in all different shapes and sizes, from the big, the bold, and the audacious, to the small, which are never very small at all. It is hard to tell from where these dreams come, but it is important to acknowledge their presence and to never ignore them. For if we are not careful, if we do not breathe life into dreams, our dreams become ghosts, forever haunting us throughout our lives.

This dream came to me when I was hunched over, bent but not broken, gasping for breath in the small time between one full field sprint and the next. Like the steam rising off of my body when heat and cold collide, these words rose up inside of me, first as a whisper and then as a roar: "I want to be an All-American." Thereafter, this was my mantra:

I AM AN ALL-AMERICAN

I ached for this the way one longs for a lover long lost or a summer since past, forsaking all else for this dream to come true. It was a yearning so great that it was metallic to taste and electric to touch for I wanted all of those days, all of those runs, all of that physical exhaustion to have counted for something.

Because of this, Jesse was the only person I told of this dream. Not soon after, he gave me a red Matchbox car with my number, 19, on the hood. In true Jesse fashion he inserted a toothpick with a handwritten banner that read *"All-American is all you."* Jesse was, is, and always will be the believer of dreams.

Season continued and this dream metamorphasized into reality with each goal scored and each game won and by the beginning of May, my dream came true: I was an All-American.

But the best of lacrosse days was Mother's Day, 2001 when we found ourselves on the eastern shore of Maryland for the second or third time that season, face to face with our biggest conference rival: Salisbury University. My parents drove down from New York and everyone's else's parents were there too. It was the end of the season and this game was make or break. If we won we would go on to the big dance, the Final Four, the National Championship. If we lost it was over, but today was no day for doubt.

As the sun appeared and disappeared behind late spring clouds we beat Salisbury. Two weeks later we went on to the Big Dance where we lost in the first round; outmatched, outran, and outplayed. But still, we were there. We had made it that far and we returned to Fredericksburg as champions, if only in our own minds, knowing this to be true in our hearts:[2]

All of our lives we search for what defines us. We try to find it

---

[2] It is such a joy to announce that at the time of this writing word was received that the Mary Washington College 2001 Woman's Lacrosse team is to be inducted into the UMW Collegiate Hall of Fame. Well done, ladies. Well done. Can't wait to see you in February!

anywhere and everywhere forgetting that who we are can be found in the places that we do not need to be anything else.

The lacrosse field is where I found myself, where I lose myself, and where I have learned everything about myself.

Every drop of rain, every bead of sweat, every tear, every goal scored, every goal missed, every yard, every mile, every second, every day, everything taught me:

To trust my instincts.

To never give up.

To rise above.

Sometimes there is no such thing as home field advantage.

To carry my burdens with ease and without complaints.

To win with humility and to lose without admitting defeat.

Dedication is sometimes met with resistance, but determination overcomes disappointment every time.

And that you cannot get anywhere in this life without moving your feet.

They will tell you to leave it all out on the field, but the field is always with you, just as the field has always been with me. For in my heart it is always lacrosse season. Just as I will always be an athlete. For me, there is no other choice.

Now, as then, as always, when someone tells me that I throw like a girl, I smile and say:

YOU BET YOUR ASS I DO!

On the Worst of Tuesdays

Tuesday, from the Latin *dies Martis*

The Day of Mars:

The God of War

In my second to last semester of senior year my schedule was such that both Amber and I had no classes on Tuesdays so Tuesdays became our favorite day of the week where Amber and I woke up late, lunched downtown, and then, since we were young, dumb, and full of fun, we drank in the middle of the afternoon and played ambitious games of beer pong on the porch of her house as our roommates drove back and forth to their classes on campus. In those first days of September, when summer was not yet stripped of her heat, we promised each other that it would always be like this and that nothing would ever change.

That Tuesday was to be no different. A few minutes before nine o'clock, maybe after, I called Amber. That was when she told me the world was on fire. In words incomprehensible she spoke of planes and buildings and fires and bombs, but I did not understand any of what she had said. I only hung up the phone and ran down two flights of stairs just in time to see

United Airlines Flight 175 fly into the South Tower. My only thoughts were these:

My sister works there. My sister works in those buildings. She is always late. She is never on time. Please let her be late today. Please let everyone be late today.

When I picked up the phone again there was no dial tone, there was no busy signal, there was only static. No one could be reached.

And so we sat, all six of us in front of the television, mute with shock, horror, and disbelief. How foolish I was to think that those buildings made of all things flammable would remain standing, that somehow, the damage was reparable and that these buildings could withstand this. And then they collapsed. Unable to watch the destruction I ran outside and up the street to where Lauren, my fellow New Yorker, my best friend, was already waiting with outstretched arms and we cried, oh how we cried.

Had I known that the 11th of September did not stand alone as a singular tragedy in the history of the Americas, perhaps I would have awoken with a little more hesitation. Had I remembered Chile in 1973, my already broken heart would break just a little bit more, for how many people are there in this world who wish that it could always remain the 10th of September?

At twenty-one I was silly enough to believe that the world was moving beyond terrorism, that the start of the new millennium might mean that there was to be no more war, no more violence, only peace. But to believe that we were infallible to these kinds of attacks was both naïve and ignorant for acts of terror had been carried out on American soil before, many of them committed by American citizens: Timothy McVeigh, Teddy Kaczynski, Eric Harris and Dylan Keibold. But their reigns of terror seemed finite and singular at the time. Something about this spoke of permanence. A world without order, a world of only continued chaos.

That night, the sky was silent, the world was silent. There were no planes and even the stars refused to shine. In the late hours, when words returned to our lips, we stood in the kitchen trying to make sense of the senselessness of it all. My roommate's boyfriend, who planned to work for the FBI after graduation, explained to us who it was that masterminded these acts of terror. It was the first time that I had heard his name, forgetting that I might have heard it in 1993, and so I repeated it over and over again, committing it to the place where only the most violent of memories reside: Osama bin Laden. Osama bin Laden. Osama bin Laden

In the days and weeks that followed the television stayed on, it was never turned off, as new developments were broadcast other pronouns began to be heard with more frequency: Al- Qaeda, Taliban, Afghanistan.

For all too brief of a time I wanted to join the army.

Si vis pacem, para bellum.

In October, I drove home to New York to be with my family. Crossing over the Verrazano Bridge, I stayed in the left lane in order to merge onto the Brooklyn Queens Expressway: a road that had always offered the best view of the Manhattan skyline. But this time, the skyline was vacant. There were no watchtowers, only emptiness, only darkness.

As I looked into the rearview mirror to stare into the void that remained only two words echoed into that autumn night: Never Again. Never Again. Never Again.

After crossing the border from Brooklyn into Queens, I remembered how, less than a year before, I was enrolled in a seminar on Elie

Weisel so as to learn what can be learned from the madness of men. At the turn of the millennia, it seemed appropriate to be studying this man at this time of great, all too great, uncertainty, for by 2001, the number of tragedies that had transpired over the course of my lifetime, over the course of a century, had already surpassed my scope of understanding. That these tragedies still continued to take place was even more devastating and it occurred to me that fifty-five years after the Holocaust nothing has been learned from war, from violence, from destruction, from killing, from death. Nothing has been learned from the words *Never Again*.

Near the end of that semester, this survivor of Auschwitz and Buchenwald came to speak to an audience of young college students who not only believed that the world could be changed, but that the world will be changed. I sat in the middle of the auditorium and listened to him tell of the unspeakable time before and after being liberated from behind the barbed wire fences of Auschwitz. That night, he reminded all of us:

If someone had told us in 1945 that in our lifetime religious wars would rage on every continent, that thousands of children would once again be dying of starvation, we would not have believed it. If someone had told us that racism and fanaticism would flourish once again, we would not have believed it.

Fifty-six years later, I still could not believe it. Even now, seventy-one years later, it is still difficult to believe.[3]

---

[3] It is with great difficulty that I write this passage as gross violations of human rights continue to occur on every continent, even now, in this very moment, without cease and seemingly without hope.

After, college went on, overshadowed as it was by an inevitable war. In the spring, lacrosse season began again and we returned once more to the Final Four, but this time it was different. This time we knew of even greater defeats and lesser victories. And so we lost in the first round of the tournament and made our bittersweet return to Fredericksburg to graduate and to begin life after college.

That May, before the heat and the humidity arrived in the South, I packed everything away: my clothes, my room, my books, everything that I had known for the past four years, and said goodbye to my house on Wolfe Street, I said goodbye to my roommates, I said goodbye to Virginia, and said hello, once again, to New York.

Once in Northport I picked up a paintbrush and a roller and went to work painting houses inside and out. After all, what is the good in studying art if you don't give it a try yourself? But Michelangelo I was not and I learned all too quickly that soffits are not the ceiling of the Sistine Chapel and it was there in Rome, and not here in Northport, that I wanted to be.

Less than a year after that fateful September morning, that Fourth of July was unlike any other even though we still did what we did every year to celebrate our independence: we sailed out into the middle of the harbor, listened to rock and roll, drank cold beers, and watched fireworks explode all around us.

Late in the afternoon, *"America the Beautiful"* rang out across the harbor and as Ray Charles sang out this beautiful melody I sat on the bow of the boat, away from the crowded stern, the most reluctant of patriots, watching the way the world carried on and even the sky was patriotic: sun red, clouds white, sea blue.

As the sun sank below the horizon, clouds gathered and the heat of July gave way to a storm building. In the distance, streaks of lightening cut through the night as claps of thunder echoed the explosions of saltpeter, sulphur, and charcoal across the sound. As we watched and waited for the rains that did not come I felt the need to distance myself from this place. My soul ached for something far away for this America was not to last. Another storm was fast approaching.

On Europe

At first it was only supposed to be Katie and I, off on our grand tour of Europe, but then Addie, my friend from high school, decided to join us, as did her friend, Joe, from college and as our twosome grew to four, so did our probability of more adventures and mishaps along the way. In those anxious exciting days before we left and stereotypically twenty-two, I fooled myself into believing that Europe was where I was going to 'find myself', as always what a fool. What a fool.

As September began we flew to London. Since Katie and I had already been there, we grew desperate to see the rest of the United Kingdom, the rest of Europe, and the rest of the world. So there we stayed for only one night, determined as we were to move on as quickly as possible.

On the tenth of September, Katie and I took an overnight bus to Edinburgh. Unable to sleep I watched the black of night surrender its darkness to the dawn as a sea of stars was replaced by the single solitary sun of morning.

In Scotland, we drank café au laits and ate a breakfast of shortbread cookies cloaked in layers of thick caramel and milk chocolate and it seemed as if the different densities of butter, milk, and sugar were in competition with one another where one bite was smooth, the next crisp, and all were sweet and crumbling just so on our lips and tongues. In these cafes we read and we wrote and we tried our damnedest to channel our inner J.K. Rowling (if only, if only). When our hands grew tired, we climbed to the top of the castle high on a hill in the center of the city. Long after the sun had set on the United Kingdom, we drank cold bottles of Stella Artois in pubs and hoped that the loves of our lives stood somewhere among the drunken strangers in the crowd.

The following day a ferry was taken to Northern Ireland where the Troubles were far from over. In a café we befriended three Irish boys from Belfast who taught us insults like: *"Yee got a face on yee like a rotweiler chewin a wasp,"* and compliments like *"We get on like a house on fire."* Despite the Troubles, it seemed as if life had yet to get the best of them. As we ordered more beers an ambulance sped by; its doors open and its siren wailing through the streets. When the shrill of the siren could be heard no more they lowered their voices and told us stories of bombs and fires, of violence and terror, of murder and revenge. But their whispers were not secrets. Maybe to us, but not to them.

In the break of day they drove us around their city and showed us the places where the most intense fighting had taken place. On the sides of houses, on the walls of churches, under the trellises of bridges there was graffiti; colorful murals that at once begged for peace and cried for war. As we drove from one monument of war to the next we did not ask if they were Protestant or Catholic, nor did they ask us. As Americans, they did not ask us to choose sides and even if they did, it would have been impossible to choose between the same god.

That afternoon they took us to a football game, but we did not go with the intention of watching the game. Instead we went to shout abuses to the fans on the other side. Luckily for us our cries went unheard. After their team won we said our goodbyes without any promises of keeping in touch or seeing one another again and Katie and I made our way to Ireland.

In Dublin I met a boy named Fiacre who had jet-black hair and fierce blue eyes and a brogue that softened my New York heart. We laughed in between sips of whiskey and kissed in between drags of cigarettes. And in between all of this, we promised to wed and have seven, maybe eight children, and name them all Fiacre; our own clan of hunter kings. But it never happened. After that night, we never saw each other again.

Upon leaving the cold and wet September city we drove through the countryside where we passed croppings of slate gray rocks, landscapes of grass so green it made itself jealous, and a devastatingly blue and open sky. We spent a night in Killarney- where it was not Christmas- and then onward around the Dingle Peninsula. At the Cliffs of Moher the sea raged against the battered walls of shale and sandstone, which that rose up from the ocean floor as the wind wailed its lamentations upon the world.

In the space between sea and sky that old violent, yet familiar thought returned, one more step, one last step was all that was necessary. But today was not the day to learn whether or not I could fly.

From the British Isles we crossed the Channel and finally we were in France. *Arriver*. To arrive. From the Anglo-French word ariver, meaning to come to land or to touch the shore. In Paris, I had arrived. Before my bags even touched the ground I ran to the Eiffel Tower, bought myself a crepe with Nutella and bananas, and sat for hours, watching the world as it passed. When the hour grew late and the sun sank along the Seine, bathing the river in flecks of gold and silver, a chill rose in the late September air sending chills of their own down my spine. Not yet used to cooler weather I stood to catch the last glimpse of light in this City of Light and then went to go find my friends.

At the hostel, Katie, Addie, and Joe sat at a high table surrounded with bottles of wine. As the room grew crowded with backpackers returning from their days of wonder and exploration, my eyes strayed from my friends to the corner of the room where he sat at a table next to the door that opened more often than it stayed closed. He had disheveled brown hair and flecks of gold in his eyes that danced in the dimming light only accentuating his olive skin, flushed as it was by a summer spent on the Mediterranean Sea. He was younger than me by three, maybe four years and he was an Australian on his gap year. I did not know any of this yet, but I was determined to learn nevertheless. After our third bottle of liquid courage was finished a smile was exchanged and then a joke and then introductions were made. These are the tiny ripples, imperceptible at first, but small surges that forever change the course of our lives.

That night, drunk on Paris, we kissed under the lights of the Eiffel Tower and promised one another that our paths would cross again, even though I was a Gentile and he most certainly was not. The next day he was gone, off to see the rest of the continent and I was off to see a garden at Giverny.

It was not long before I discovered that I do not travel well with others. I walk fast and lack the special kind of patience that is required when knowing only one other person in the world. But it could not be helped, overcome as I was by the overwhelming desire to go everywhere and to do everything all at once. So from France we all went our separate ways for a spell: Katie to Interlocken, Addie back to America for a week, only to return to Europe, and I to Valenciennes to spend some time with Lauren who was there in the north of France teaching English for the year.

Just as the summer of September was fading we spent our days eating crepes filled with chevre and chanterelles as the goat cheese melted around mushrooms so tender that it was easy to forget that they were there. For dessert we drank *chocolat chaud,* the liquid so thick that it coated our cups and our lips with a sweetness that lingered long after we had finished. After dinner we walked arm in arm along the streets, knowing that this was the way that our friendship would always be; forever standing side by side no matter where we were in the world. The weekend passed all too quickly. On Monday, Lauren had to return to teaching and I boarded a train bound for Munich to find Katie and Addie and Joe once again. It was October, after all.

There, the beer halls of Munich are larger than American football fields and louder than any given Sunday. So as to not miss a single moment we stood on benches drinking liter after liter of beer. Drunk and loud we sang, *"Hey! Hey baby! Ooh. Ah,"* with the whole delirious crowd. How easy it was to get lost in the madness. But in Germany, there were sober moments as well.

Here, in the heart of the Holocaust, we visited the concentration camp at Dachau, which was located so close to the city center that is was hard to believe that what had taken place in this camp had gone unnoticed in the world beyond the barbed wire. But then again here in this place where work sets you free, the gas chamber was never used. There were other ways. As we walked through the barracks and the crematorium it was difficult not to question what evil lies in the hearts of men. Unsurprisingly, we found little to celebrate that night.

From Germany, we crossed over the Alps into Italy. In Florence we drove past the Duomo after midnight, where specks of the green, black, and white marble glittered in the streetlights. I wanted to stop the cab and run my fingers along the walls of this cathedral of the quatrrocento and reach up for Brunelleschi's Dome, but the hour was late and surely this Cattedrale di Santa Maria del Fiore, which after already standing for six hundred years, would surely still be there in the morning.

Besides, there was the Uffizi first to visit. And so I rose with the sun to stand in line long before the museum was to open. In those early hours I watched people walk through this corridor of history where once walked Lorenzo di Medici, Michelangelo Buonarroti, and Dante Alghieri. I imagined how the bonfire of the vanities must have raged and burned in the Piazza della Signoria during Carnivale, 1497. Even more sinister, I looked up to the windows above and imagined the wicked deaths of those punished for their participation in the Pazzi conspiracy. But mostly, I imagined young *David* being presented to his city for the first time, a boy about to face a giant, an imperfect block, gazing into the distance all too aware of his fate:

defeat or be defeated.

Once inside the Uffizi, I did as Stendhal did and wept, not in front of Caravaggio, but Botticelli. There, upon seeing *The Annunciation* for the first time my world finally fell silent and I remained both breathless and fearful that I will never again witness beauty such as this. Here, on a framed wooden panel the delicate outlines of Mary's gossamer veil and the cloak and wings of Gabriel impart the words left unspoken between the two. Stand close enough and you can sense her hesitation, his insistence. Stand close enough and you just might begin to believe in God.

Some of my family are blessed enough to call Florence their home. These are not so distant relatives who live in a house on the other side of the Arno, just west of the Ponte Vecchio. And so, not ready to leave this medieval city, I stayed with them for a few days. In the afternoon we drove to Siena and back and at night we ate meals that began after nine and did not end until well after midnight. As we moved from wine to espresso I tried to understand what it was they were saying in between fierce gesticulations and laughter that sprung from their souls, but the wine had gone to my head and I could not understand a single word.

In Florence I wanted to stay, but the history that drove me back also propelled me forward to Rome. On the road that led to Rome I met another American named Jenny. Once arrived in the Eternal City we walked to doors of the Pantheon, arm in arm, like Dorothy and her motley crew approaching the City of Oz. But what could we ask for from the Wizard that was not already ours?

After, we wandered along the sacred way of the forum and danced amid the ruins of buried and unburied history. Before returning to our hostel we stood in front of the coliseum as cars passed shining their modern headlights onto the ancient amphitheater. It was there, in the shadows of

127

history, that Jenny leaned in to ask: "*What? Did the Romans just get together one day and say, 'Let's just fucking build, let's just fucking build really big things?*" Apparently they had.

We spent the whole of the next day not in Rome, but in Vatican City. In the Stanza della Segnatura, we stood in front of centuries of philosophers and poets, scholars and students, and in the sculpture gardens I wept at the sight of Lacoon and his sons forever frozen in fear of Greeks bearing gifts. Always a sinner, rarely a saint, I kept my head down as I entered from the rear entrance of the crowded room of the Sistine Chapel until I stood below the creation. And then, I finally looked up, but I did not speak. What words are there to say in a moment such as this?

After, we descended the Spanish Steps and sat at the bottom drinking large bottles of Peroni as the sun warmed our bodies and our souls. There, we watched as people went up and down the stairs. When the seven hills of Rome were shrouded in darkness, we found *La Boca Della Verita*, but the gates were locked and the truth remained hidden from us that night.

In the early hours of morning and the fading warmth of autumn I pushed further east to Hungary. In Eastern Europe the landscape shifted: one side fertile earth, the other almost barren. It might have only been that it was now almost the end of October and the season for growth was finished, or it might have been an indication of what life was like behind the Eastern Bloc. But then again, this was life after the iron curtain was lifted. Maybe I wanted to see it as such, a visible validation that WE were right and THEY were wrong, but not everything is so transparent and most of the time it is difficult to tell the difference between the two.

When I arrived in the capital, lions stood guard on the Chain Bridge that connects Buda and Pest and on both sides of the river I walked into churches, small chapels, and orthodox cathedrals that rose up on either side never knowing what it was that I was hoping to find within their walls that could not be found within the walls of my own heart.

At the end of October, faced with the choice of going east to the castle of Vlad Tepes for the Eve of All Saints or north to Slovakia so as to see Oscar, my young Australian friend, I chose not to believe in preternatural things and boarded a train bound for Bratislava. When I arrived at the station, late after a long day of traveling, he was there waiting for me and off we went into the night.

In the days that followed we walked along the blue river and throughout the cobblestone streets of the old city where statues, cast in silver and bronze rose from beneath manhole covers and tipped their hats as we passed. Maybe we held hands. Maybe we did not touch at all. Maybe we waltzed along the Danube. Maybe we did not dance at all. Maybe this was all just a dream.

Before the arrival of winter we found ourselves in Stary Smokovec, a small town at the base of the Tatras. Outside of our hotel there was no sun, only clouds, and the coldness of early November that came too soon. For days, fog permeated the air making nothing visible except for one another. But on the morning of our departure the clouds lifted and we saw, for the first time, the mountains that surrounded us, their peaks white and jagged, closer than we had imagined and taller too. As we waited for the train it began to snow, no more than a flurry. As a New Yorker I would have thought nothing of it had it not been Oz's first time seeing snow and for him, this was magic, but like the ephemeral snowflakes that surrounded us, this moment would never happen again. The train arrived and the moment melted away.

It was not soon after that we found ourselves sitting underneath a map of the world and saw with our own eyes just how far from Australia

America lies. Then the spell was broken and we went our separate ways. When it came to developing the photographs of our time together, all of the pictures were blurry, as if my camera knew what I did not; that it was only an autumn romance and no more.

And so, forever wanting to follow in my father's footsteps, I went to Amsterdam where I made my way to the Rijksmuseum in order to stand in front of Rembrandt's *The Night Watch* (or *The Shooting Company of Frans Banning Cocq and Willem van Ruytenburch)* just as he had all of those years before. Impossible to miss, I stood in the shadows of this painting and wondered: Was it the same spot? Was it the same day? The same hour? It was hard to tell, but here I was, over forty years later asking history to repeat itself.

Here was where was learned what no art history class is able to prepare you for: that these paintings are massive and that there is no one way to describe the way they shine when the light hits them at certain angles at certain times of the day, sometimes blinding, sometimes illuminating, and they most certainly do not prepare you for how insignificant you become in their presence, as if it is these paintings that are alive and you are not.

But this painting was too big, too dark, too much. So I left the room in which it is hung and found a smaller room with smaller paintings, but only in size and not in meaning. It was there that hung *Jeremiah Lamenting the Destruction of Jerusalem*, no bigger than the palm of my hand or the page of a book. Here, a man mourns what he had foreseen but could do nothing to prevent. In the distance the city burns and alone, he grieves in silence.

After all, who are prophets, but mere mortals unwilling to accept the fate of man?

By the middle of November, funds were dwindling, or rather plummeting, and Thanksgiving was only a week away. It was time to go home. Ten weeks had passed. Ten pounds were gained. I flew back to New York, already ready to leave again.

On the Building of Houses

Anxious to get back out into the world, but needing money to do so, I searched for a job bound in freedom and not constraints. Of course I could have applied for a job in the city and put my art history degree to good use, but, as always, I was weary of conformity and in fear of falling deaf to the beating of my gypsy heart.

For the past two summers my brother Chris had worked for a builder named Peter while I babysat his three children. With my brother away at college in Massachusetts, Peter was in need of a laborer and I was in need of work so construction it was and why the hell not?

At twenty-three years old, (at twenty-four and twenty-five, and up until I had grown wise enough to realize how foolish of an endeavor this might have been) I was still out to prove that girls could do anything that boys can do, and being so young and having read so many magazines that offered contrarian advice regarding femininity, I still felt it necessary to be considered "one of the boys" and it is only now that I realize just how unnecessary this actually is. But still, this dichotomy between being and belonging, strength and vulnerability, masculine and feminine, defined the seasons of my youth and it took a long while to learn that while we are all home to these oppositions, I also needed to learn that women neither need compare themselves with men nor try to be like them, for it is our

135

differences that make us stronger, not weaker, contradistinct, not better.

What began as the painting of houses evolved into the pouring of foundations, the hanging of doors, the extending of decks, and eventually the building of homes. At first, I was the grunt, getting coffee in the morning, lunch in the afternoon, and running back and forth to the lumberyard throughout the day to pick up all that was needed for the job. But as time went on, I learned how to swing a hammer and a sledgehammer, I learned to measure twice and cut once, and eventually I learned to overcome my fear of a sawzall, because, frankly, there is just no better way to take down a plaster wall, cut through rebar, and do just about everything else that needs dismantling. But that was only later.

That January, the temperatures fell below freezing and did not rise again until spring and snow covered the frozen ground from the first snowfall until the last. In Muttontown we worked on a house without insulation, without sheetrock, and without floors. Its bones were bare. In this barren landscape of a house with only a frame and no walls, I swept away the wood shavings and only after plywood covered beams of varying widths did I fill the now framed walls with insulation as bits of fiberglass scratched the surface of my cheeks and the underbelly of my forearm. As months passed I carried sheets of gypsum through these rooms even though I was terrible at hanging them. To be fair I learned on metal studs and I had not acquired the patience necessary to rock a wall, which was new and strange to me because I had no problem finding studs anywhere else in my life.

When the ground began to thaw and the snow began to melt, we started demolition. Then it was easy to fall in love with destruction. It was easy to fall in love with sledgehammers and jackhammers, crowbars and pry bars. So that spring I fell in love with tearing things down only to be rebuilt.

At the end of May, my brother Chris returned to work for Peter and the twins who lived around the corner from our house joined our crew. In the middle of summer, when the air grew so thick with humidity that it seemed to stand still, we stood on roofs and watched the heat as it rose over the eaves. In unabating heat we stripped the shingles down to the plywood as the tar stuck to our gloves and left streaks of black across our already ruined clothes. And despite how dirty I was at the end of the day this manual labor was one of the most humbling of experiences for it offered of a sense of accomplishment unfound in any other job I had held until them. But these senses of accomplishment were not without their defeats.

One early morning in March, Peter and I drove west on 25A as the sun grew bold and crept over the hills to melt what snow remained in late spring. In these moments of new light our conversations turned to politics and politicians, the fate of America and the fate of the world. From the passenger seat I spoke out against the President and the war that had just begun in Iraq, unable to understand how, after millenniums of fighting, we still sought answers in violence. What lesson has not yet been learned from war that we must continue to hazard into it again and again? Peter's answer was always the same: *"You are young and a bleeding heart liberal. When you get to be my age you will begin to see the world a little differently. Remember, you can't change the world."*

I tried to raise my voice in protest, forever desiring, like Doctor Martin Luther King Jr., to see the world not as it is, but how it ought to be, but I allowed myself to be crippled by the notion that perhaps he was right: the world cannot be changed. And so we sat in the forced disquiet of the cab listening to fear's lullabies that slowly put down to an uneasy and fitful sleep the dreams of a better world, not by song, but by silence.

Despite our political differences I worked for Peter through the spring and into the summer, saving all of the money needed for my next adventure: China.

And why China? One might think that it was because it is a country so vast that it spans five geographical time zones despite its unification under Beijing time or because it is a landscape full of deserts and mountains, tundra and tropics. Or maybe it is because its history is as dense as it is deep. Or maybe only because it is there and sometimes you need to travel to a place so grand and so long lasting just to be reminded how determined life is to go on despite how often the bell that is meant to signal the end of the world is rung.

Maybe it was all of these things, but closer to the truth, it was none of these things. It was simply because of a small sign in a hostel in Dublin that advertised an opportunity to teach English in China. After reading it for less than a second I thought, "*Oh, all right, if I must.*" So easily swayed, that was all it took.

On Hawaii

My flight for China was to depart so very early on some arbitrary August day so since it was not known how long I was to be gone, we went out for one last night of debauchery, we being my sisters Kristen, Michele, my brother Chris, and my friends: Heather, Addie, and Rob. All together we drank (too much), we took shots (too many), we sang (perhaps too loud), and we stayed out (too late or just late enough to not have to set an alarm in order to wake up the next morning). In hindsight this was not the best of ideas for someone about to board a plane in just a few hours, but life lends itself ever so generously to mistakes. How else are we to learn?

Hung over, or still drunk, I left for China with a one-way ticket in my hand and a practically visible chip on my shoulder. Some may have called it my propensity towards drapetomania, which was not so far from the truth because it was always easier to run away from the life that I had not yet grown comfortable in living rather that muster the courage necessary to look into the sometimes brutal, sometimes beautiful, and forever truthful mirror of my heart.

But it was also more than that: it was an unquenchable desire to measure the width and depth of my soul. For we do not always grow by establishing our roots, sometimes we can only grow by spreading our wings.

When my parents, bless their hearts, who had supported me my entire life, were kind enough to give me a ride to the airport, I demonstrated my gratitude by saying to them: "Goodbye. I don't really know when I am coming back again, so I guess I'll see you around..."

Unfiltered, I neither gave thought to the weight of these words, nor cared about the damage that they may cause. What an ungrateful and downright ratchet bitch I was. Here I was, flesh of their flesh and blood of their blood saying the most awful things a child can say to their parents. So maybe it was that they were as happy to see me go as I was to leave. Once through the gates I did not look back. Not. Even. Once.

Needless to say, I did not win the award for *Daughter of the Year* in 2003.

My flight to China had a pit stop, not because the flight to China is so damn long, but because there were other histories in need of visiting before visiting China. And sometimes, in order to move forward, we must also regress.

Over Christmas break of my senior year of college I returned home to find a Hawaiian calendar on the dresser of my mother's room. It seemed out of place amid her pearls and *Lladros*. Forever curious, I leaned on her bed flipping through photographs of honu turtles, Waikiki sunsets, and the lava flows of Mauna Loa and each month was more colorful than the last. January. February. By March, she told me to sit down. There was something that she needed to tell me. There was something that I needed to know. This calendar told a story over fifty years old of a young man who fought for his country during the second World War, a man who was stationed in the South Pacific for its duration, and a man who, after the war ended, returned to New York, never to go back to Hawaii again. It was the story of a soldier before he became a husband and a father. It was the story of my grandfather.

The phone call came some months or weeks before. They called almost all of the Chirichella's in the phone book before they found who it was they were looking for. A man named John made the phone call at the insistence of his wife so that he could perhaps set his father's mind and heart at ease. He called to tell my mother a story that she had never heard before, not because it was new, but because it had been kept a secret for all of these years. Before hanging up the phone my mother learned two things:

She had a brother.
Her father had a son.

Perhaps my mother's prayers for a big family were finally answered after all.

Small wonder that *Mele Kelikimaka* was our favorite Christmas song as children. This story had already been borne in our bones.

In August I flew to Oahu as the ambassador of my family, the one who would represent all of us to our Hawaiian family. Perhaps my dreams of being a diplomat had finally come true after all, but Lord knows what the rest of them were thinking.

In the weeks before I left I watched *Lilo and Stitch* where I learned that: "*In Hawaiian, Ohana means family and family means no one gets left behind.*" But sometimes people do get left behind. They may not be forgotten, but behind they remain nevertheless.

At the airport she smiled. Without ever having met her, I knew who she was: my Auntie Kilani, the wife of my Uncle John. In her hands she carried a plumeria lei, its petals magenta and white, its aroma soft and sweet and she draped the floral necklace over my shoulders before kissing both of my cheeks. Outside my Uncle John waited for us with the car, but I did not need her to point him out because he looked almost exactly like his father. Had I never known that my grandfather had a son and had I met my uncle in any other circumstance I would still wonder at the sight of him. He was tall, but not too tall. He was serious, but not too serious. And he was handsome, just like his father.

In English, Oahu means 'gathering place.' And here, in this place of gathering I met my cousins, all boys: John, Christian, and Bungee, all with children of their own. From the very beginning, they took me in as their own. After all, Ohana means family.

Late in the evening, after the fires of the hibachi cooled, we drank beers as my cousins strummed their ukuleles and sung Hawaiian songs that told of myths and legends, kings and queens, wars and warriors. When their voices began to fade, the trade winds carried their songs through the palm trees and out into the ocean.

Along this ring of fire, we hiked volcanoes not long dormant and visited the place where King Kamehameha united all of the Hawaiian Islands as one kingdom. We came to the place where the Queen of Hawaii, Lili'uokalani, was forced to abdicate her thrown at the behest of the American government. So as to prevent the shedding of blood she conceded perhaps knowing all the while that sugar is not that sweet. We did as the tourists do and surfed Waikiki Beach, and then we did as the locals do and ate poke, tofu, shaved ice, and even spam. We spent a Sunday afternoon in Waimanalo diving off of a small boat as sea turtles and kikakapu swam in the clear clear waters and the Kaupo cliffs rose stoically behind us. As the day offered itself to the night, we waded into the Pacific Ocean, the sky aflame in pinks and oranges, the water expanding in all directions beyond obsidian and coral reefs. On the last day of this journey we went to Pearl Harbor, to the place where this story begins. Here the wreckage of the USS Arizona sleeps soundly below the surface, sometimes visible, sometimes obscured by view in the rising and falling of the tide. I tried to imagine that infamous day, but it is difficult to imagine the way in which war begins and even more difficult to imagine war's end.

After midnight, when the house grew quiet and even the winds grew still, I lay awake wondering just how many sons were born to fathers that they were never to meet? How many men left for war not knowing if and when they would ever come back? Does the world, during these all too tumultuous times, somehow seek balance between all the lives lost and new life just begun? Only one thing was certain:

War leaves nothing unchanged, nothing untouched.
And sometimes, even in war, there is no difference between winning and losing.
War is war is war is war.

Although I was there for less than a week, it seemed as if a whole lifetime was lived and a piece of the puzzle, long missing, was put into place. Before I left I made promises that I was not certain that I could keep since it was not my place to guarantee that one day my grandfather would meet his son. And still, I promised nevertheless.

145

On China

Before leaving for China, I knew only two phrases in Mandarin: *Ni Hao* and *Wo ai ni*, so I imagined myself going around as Jim Morrison might have done, telling everyone, "Hello, I love you," except in Chinese.

Do not ask me why it is that I do not think it is important to have a place to stay the moment your feet touch the ground in a foreign country where you don't speak a lick of the language in the middle of the night. Maybe it is my fear of all that is set in stone or maybe it is my sweet embrace of both the knowing that not all goes according to plan and faith that sometimes things seem to work out exactly as they should.

Luckily, I happened to be sitting next to another female traveller on the plane who offered the other bed in her hotel room. All of a sudden, my father's fears that his daughter just might get sold into white slavery returned until just after our plane took off and she said only this: *"Here we go, off to our little dreams."* Once again, another angel was in my midst.[4]

Once through customs we hailed a cab to take us into the city center. The hour was late, or early depending on which clock was looked at, and soon we fell asleep (in the safety of our shared hotel room), where there was no need to dream for our dreams had just come true.

---

[4] Let it be known that the author does not condone this type of behavior while traveling. In other words: do not try this at home and, more importantly, do not try this abroad.

In the morning we stepped out into the world that is China. All at once, a sea of cyclists swarmed around us and the whir of their tires and the click, click, click of their pedals only added to the almost deafening cacophony of Beijing. Their baskets were full of produce, briefcases, and sometimes even small children who waved frantically at us as if seeing white women was yet not an everyday occurrence for them. Most wore surgical masks on their faces in the hopes of preventing the transmission of SARS, which was still a threat throughout Asia, but not enough of a deterrent from traveling there. Along the avenues, broad and narrow, women carried umbrellas to shelter themselves from the sun as men walked arm and arm down the streets. Everywhere hung larger than life posters of the Great Mentor, the Great Helmsman, the Great Commander: Mao Tse Tong. Each of these photographs was a not so subtle reminder of the Cultural Revolution that had swept through China from 1966 to 1976. But this was not a time to think about this or what it would mean for me as an American about to live in a Communist country- at least not yet- for our bellies rumbled and as always with me, empty stomachs and deep historical thoughts do not go hand in hand. Somewhere along these streets a woman beckoned us into her restaurant where we feasted on dumplings and noodles and sipped on steaming cups of cha. It was a breakfast so very different than the pancakes and egg sandwiches that had been left behind.

When we were fully sated I said goodbye to my brief travelling companion, thanking her for her hospitality, and boarded another plane to Xi'an, where I was to teach English. We flew over mountains, an ocean of hills that rippled like waves crashing into one another forming ever-higher peaks over the breathtaking landscape.

At the airport of Xi'an I was met by four student teachers responsible for taking me to the school and my future apartment. They were
150

all no more than eighteen and no more fluent in English than I was in Chinese. In the van they sat lighting cigarette after cigarette, laughing and speaking in a language I could not even begin to comprehend. But they were young and vibrant and brimming with excitement for their lives and their city, which was all too contagious until I caught a glimpse of the nuclear power plant that rose up in the distance, ominous and somber against a purple and polluted sky.

As a teacher of foreign language housing was to be provided for me in the form of my own apartment close to the city center. But when I arrived I was told that I would be sharing an apartment with two Chinese students who were studying to be teachers. A red flag was raised, but it was not the banner of the People's Republic of China.

But still, that evening we walked through the Muslim quarter of Xi'an where stalls lined the streets and men, young and old, peddled wares said to be as old as the Silk Road itself. Here, in this ancient corridor that has withstood falls of empires and invasion from all directions we were to have dinner with the faculty of the school.

In the restaurant, red lanterns lit the otherwise darkened room and we sat close together at a round table as the principal ordered dish after dish of meats, vegetables, and mysteries. This meal, the first of many shared meals in China, was full of food and customary practices unparalleled and unrivaled, even in my Italian family. Rice wine (*mijiu*) was brought to the table and salutes of *Gan Bei* were offered before emptying the small glass of that sweet cool liquid. Unwilling to lose face I ate everything that was placed before me believing myself to be both strong of will and fierce of stomach, but just how strong that was, was only to be determined the next morning.

That night, back at my apartment, as the fluorescent light drowned all other color from the room, I stared at the bare blank chalk walls,

151

wondering just how it was that I had arrived in this place. On the one hand I felt expectant, privileged, and full of too much pride and not enough humility given the circumstances, but on the other hand, I also felt disoriented and uncertain as to whether I had made the best of decisions.

Ever willing to make the best of the situation that I had now found myself, I set out to explore Xi'an, the city of 'Perpetual Peace,' the next morning. It is said that Xi'an, at its height, rivaled the likes of Athens, Rome, and Constantinople and it is here, where antiquity meets modernity, that pagodas stand side by side with skyscrapers and American happy meals are served alongside of *Mei Fan.*

When I came upon the Great Mosque, I walked in hesitantly, uncertain as to whether or not I would be welcomed inside of its gates. A *paifang* marked the entrance and the walls of the temple were decorated with inscriptions from the Quran written in both Arabic and Hanzi. From the minaret a muezzin called the faithful to prayer. As a "Christian" and out of respect, I departed quietly eager to see what more this city had to offer. But I did not get far before I was reminded that I had eaten foreign food in a foreign land and now it was time to reap what had been sown. At first there was just a slight discomfort and then a feeling, not of nausea, but something else, something far more dire. This feeling had been felt before, but always within a safe distance of a bathroom. But here I was in an ancient city without toilet paper and without a toilet- at least by Western standards- and with only one thought in my head:

I am going to shit my pants.

So I did as any athlete would do at such a desperate time as this; from the city center I sprinted all the way to my apartment, through throngs of Xi'an residents, dodging taxis, street merchants, and the occasional stray animal that so much as dared to cross my path. Deeply determined, I said my own prayers along the way:

I CANNOT shit my pants.
I WILL NOT shit my pants.

Somehow, someway, I made it.

I DID NOT shit my pants.

Before school was to begin a trip was taken with all of the students to a place that can only be likened to the Versailles of Xi'an where there were sprawling gardens, idyllic and serene, horses in pasture, and even a palace of the twentieth century. In the shade we ate ice cream and watched as the children played their summer games in the days before they had to return to school.

That night the intervention of fate came in the form of two Nigerian men, younger than I and all the more ready to experience a world so very different from their own. In their living room we sat speaking of the lands that we left behind. They, too, were to be teachers at this school, but their visas had not yet been processed, even though they had already been in Xi'an for over a month, and each day the fine for their unfiled paperwork that was to be completed by the school was increasing significantly and if more time were to pass they would have to leave China and return to Nigeria without having taught a single class. At that moment nothing seemed right. More red flags were raised. And I knew then that this was not where I was supposed to be.

Despite the twelve-hour time difference between New York and China, I called my mother crying, scared, and awaiting the "I told you so" that never came. I did not know what to do. Only she did. My mother always knew what to do. And despite what I had said only a few days before, my mother picked up the phone and listened as she always has. After twenty-three years, my mother had long grown used to the trouble that her daughter seemed to get herself into and, as always, she calmed me down for she is the perpetual problem solver: catastrophe is her specialty.

After the panic had subsided I remembered another organization that I had spoken with before departing for China and after contacting them, I was placed in another school, even after so short of notice. Never in my life have I packed so fast and departed so quickly.

Years later, when I looked back on these days, I realize that although this clash between fantasy and reality sometimes seems cataclysmic, more often than not, it is a not a curse, but a blessing offering lessons in humility and resilience and courage. And since then, that is how I have gotten through all of my days: humble, resilient, and most of all, courageous.

Following my mother's always sage advice, I booked a ticket to Guilin and hightailed it out of Xi'an. But before I left, I visited the Terracotta Army in their resting place in the necropolis of Qin Shi Huang. These protectors of an ancient realm, rediscovered less than three decades before, stood at attention in the vast and enclosed space. Clay figures upon clay earth, these warriors seemed both strong and delicate and as I looked upon their broken and not so broken figures I felt as if it was I who was

Humpty Dumpty sitting upon a wall, but I was not yet ready to have a great fall.

As the sun began to break through the purple clouds of the city, I hailed a cab to get me to the airport so that a plane could take me far away from the almost mess that I had gotten myself into.

Fei ji chang (airport): the third phrase I learned in Mandarin.
Xie Xie (thank you): the fourth.

I arrived in Guilin at night, always at night, but this time with a ride from the airport and a place to stay. Outside of the gates the air was heavy for summer had not yet given up its ranks. When I first saw the palm trees decorated with neon lights I knew that I had come to the right place and, like Annie when she first entered the Warbuck Mansion, I wanted to break out in song (and dance) and tell the whole of Guilin how much I knew I was gonna like it there, but it was not time to celebrate just yet.

Once collected from the airport we drove to Yangzhou in silence under a canopy of stars, the clouds no more than veils behind which revealed dark shadows rising tall and narrow in the distance. The hour was late and the road was almost empty save for the small storefronts lit by both small fires and artificial light. Above shined clusters of stars and constellations: Pleiades, Lyra, the band of the Milky Way, and Polaris. And although the night skiy may not have changed, everything below had and I grew ever so curious to see what the light of morning would reveal.

The next day, the thirtieth of August 2003, I turned twenty-three years old. This was to be the first birthday that I was to spend alone and in the morning I was awakened by a cacophony of noises: the barking of a dog, the cry of a child, and the shouts of merchants along the streets. After dressing, I made my way to the world that awaited me. Once outside, the light of the sun transformed the shadows of night into mountains that sprang from the landscape like giants awakening from an ancient sea slumber; how the yawned and stretched their monolithic limbs.

Forever a New Yorker, I weaved in and out of the crowded streets searching, always searching, for a place to feed my insatiable hunger. Soon, the chaos gave way to calm and a restaurant was found with outdoor seating and I ordered a breakfast of chrysanthemum mint tea and banana pancakes. When the last of the crepes were eaten and only petals and sodden sprigs remained in the ceramic pot I moved on to climb eight hundred steps of rocks and concrete slabs that led to the top of Moon Hill. An elderly woman, who had done this many times before kept me company, offering water and a place to rest my feet along the way if she felt that I had grown too tired. Determined, I did not stop until the trees grew sparse and an ancient circle, as old as the peaks themselves, widened and became an oculus, offering a bewildering view of Yangzhuo and the world beyond. Here, at the top of the world I watched as Li River threaded through the karst peaks in the valley below where, from their sampans and skiffs, fisherman cast their nets into the water as their doulis shading their eyes from the late summer sun. It was only then, looking down from the moon upon this earthly realm, that this beauty, unanticipated wondrous beauty, became my expectation for all birthdays to come, even though I knew that this moment was never to be repeated, not even once, and so I descended knowing that this was to always remain the best of birthdays.

On the stairwell of the hotel, fate intervened once again; for it was there that I met Nina, a Brit from Birmingham who spoke the Queen's

English. She was an elementary school teacher, a year older than I, who had just arrived by way of Russia and Mongolia on the Trans Siberian Railway. Together we learned that we were both to teach in Guilin and for the first time since arriving in China, I did not feel so alone and that this was exactly where I was supposed to be.

At week's end I was taken to Guilin and introduced to Benjamin, the principal of Qing Feng Xie Xiao, who had learned how to speak English by listening to the Beatles, which is really the only way to learn English and he spent the whole of the afternoon singing songs off of Help! and the White Album as he gave me the grand tour of the school and the apartment that I was to call my own, a privilege anywhere in the world. This apartment was spacious, grandiose even, with windows in every room that looked out into the courtyard below and the schoolyard beyond. There was a television and a DVD player, a computer, and even a washing machine; all unexpected luxuries, but appreciated nonetheless. But the best part about this apartment was not the amenities that it came with, but the saloon doors that divided the bathroom from the rest of the apartment and a showerhead, which stood directly over the western toilet. It was perfect and it was now home.

Before school was to begin I was asked to go to the hospital for a physical examination. In the most surreal of experiences I lay on a hospital bed while a Chinese doctor, speaking in French, measured my pulse and blood pressure. At first, her fingers pressed gently along my radial artery, but displeased with her findings she told me that my pulse was too slow. *Was it because I was white?* She wondered. Forever a student of medicine and curious as to whether or not her theory held sway, she asked me to run up and down the stairs and through the darkened hallways of the hospital for ten to fifteen minutes just to make sure that my low resting heart rate was not too great of a concern. Unable to explain to her that it was my athleticism that kept my heart beat low and that it had nothing to do with the color of my skin, up and down the stairs I went until perspiration formed along my brow and I was sufficiently 'warmed up' with a heart rate elevated to a more appropriate Far Eastern level. Maybe she was just taking the piss out of me or maybe it was just that she wanted to see the extent of a white woman's craziness, but when she took my pulse again she seemed pleased with her findings and passed my physical.

That weekend, as new teachers to the city of Guilin, Nina and I were invited to celebrate the Full Moon Festival at the Guilin Botanical Garden. There, we met the mayor and ate moon cakes; those small treats filled with red bean paste and decorated with geometric patterns that told of ancient legends and lore that are eaten in reverence of Chang'e and there, among the stone and steel sculptures, that we celebrated the fullness of the Harvest Moon. Thereafter, my time in Guilin was measured by the cycles of the moon; where days were marked by perigee and apogee, waxing and waning, fullness and newness, and change, forever change.

On the first day in the classroom there they were, sixty students sitting side-by-side, row-by-row. It was intimidating to see all of those eyes, all one hundred and twenty of them, staring at me, expecting me to teach them a language that I had not yet mastered, the depths of which I still had yet to understand. If truth were told, I had no idea what I was doing for I had traveled well beyond my element. Besides, an online course in TEFL does little to prepare you for these moments. So we began with introductions that went something like this:

"Hello. My name is Li Xiu Ying and in my family there is my mother, my father, and I. I am only child."

On and on it went from student to student and although their names were different, their family structure was always the same. In the haste of beginning another adventure I had forgotten that China, in order to limit the growth of its population, which had by then swelled to one quarter of the world's population, allowed only one child to be born to each family. They were all only children.

At first, because of limitations in language, it was necessary to take buses everywhere and a bus line ran from *Fei Ji Guang Chung* into the city center. But as time passed and more Chinese was learned I eventually gathered the courage to climb on the back of a motorcycle- that fantastic form of transportation that allows for freedom unfound in buses and taxis and all else that separates you from the rest of the world. In the beginning, unused to vehicles with no windows, no doors, and only two wheels, I held on tight, fearful of every bump, every turn, and every chicken that crossed the road for absolutely no reason. But before long, I loosened my grip on the strap and learned to lean into every turn. Eventually I encouraged the driver to cut through all of the alleys and short cuts knowing that not only were these routes faster, but they were a hell of a lot more fun.

Most days, my destination was the supermarket, which I went to, not always because I was hungry, but out of culinary curiosity. In the produce section there were fruits and vegetables, the likes of which had never seen before. But the real adventure lay in the meat department. In this aisle of the grocery store were found the brains and stomachs and tongues of cows, the hearts and intestines of pigs, thousand year-old eggs and chicken's feet: all entrails and viscera, blood and bones. But I did not buy any of it, partly because I was uncertain how to prepare much of it, but also because I lack the patience required to 'wait in line' at the check out counter, for to stand in line in China is to quickly realize that there are no lines in China. You must surrender order and accept chaos. There is no other way. So there these meats stayed in their cooler awaiting the hands of someone more inclined to take on such delicacies. Besides, most of my real food shopping was done in the outdoor markets of *Fei Ji Guang Chung*, where the produce tumbled from the stands and spilt out onto the street. There, dried chili peppers were spread on blankets and tarps, loose leaves of tea were sold by the handful, and herbal remedies said to cure whatever ailment one might have could be found. On tables, apples and clementines and pomegranates and small bunches of small bananas, some no larger than the size of my hand, were stacked next to spices of every name and color. In almost all of the stalls there were flowers, which were bought every week and kept in a vase by the kitchen sink to brighten even the greyest of days. And when I did not feel like cooking I ate the Guilin *Mei fan* that simmered in street carts ready to be served at a moments notice and eaten just as quickly.

Soon after, Saturday mornings became my favorite day to teach. Most of the older students did not have class and I was left with the younger students, all not yet teenagers, which made them more playful and less serious than their older counterparts. In the last few moments of class we played games like Mother May I? and Eye Spy With My Little Eye. In a world so full of color, it was a game with no end. We guessed the blue of the sky, the green of the grass, the brown of our eyes, and then one color among all other colors was picked: YELLOW. But it was not the sun or the walls of the classroom that had been chosen for this turn. Apparently it was none of these things. It was something else. The children guessed and guessed until one boy, the one who wore the sweater from which the color yellow was found, hazarded an answer with the self assurance of a boy who can do no wrong by pointing to his own skin and saying: "*Laoshi, this, this is yellow.*" Immediately, the whole classroom erupted in laughter. Where and when he learned this, I do not know, except that it was not from me. By then, I had lived in China for three months and I had seen men, women and children with so many different skin colors, some dark, some light, that it never occurred to me to deem them 'yellow.'[5] When class ended, the children were still laughing as they pointed to my skin and called it yellow as well.

"*Laoshi, Laoshi, ni shi Zhong guo ren.*"
"*Wo bu shi Zhong guo ren.*"
"*Shi de! Shi de!*"

"Teacher, Teacher, you are Chinese."
"No, I am not Chinese."
"Yes you are! Yes you are!"

I tried to raise my voice in protest, but it was not to be heard. Small of

---

[5] But then again, there was one day in the square where a man came up to me and began to speak to me as if we had known each other for quite some time. When I told him that we did not he apologized and said, "*All of you white people look the same to me.*" Closer to the truth, Chinese are referred to as "yellow" not because of the color of their skin, but due to the fact that Chinese civilization developed around the Yellow River and most Chinese can trace their descent back to the time of the Huang (Yellow) Empire.

stature and lean of frame, if it were not for the curls in my hair and the shape of my eyes, maybe I could be mistaken for Chinese. Maybe we are not so different after all.

On Thursdays, a car arrived in the early hours of the morning to take me to a school over an hour away. In the cramped space of the cab, the driver smoked cigarette after harsh cigarette and rolled the window down just enough for the ashes, and the ashes alone, to escape. We did not speak, not because we did not want to, but because we could not; the words that I knew in Chinese and the words that he knew in English were not enough to sustain a conversation. So we drove in silence except for the all too occasional blare of the horn as we passed car after car and my sharp intake of breath that could be heard as we veered in and out of traffic, more often heading into oncoming traffic than staying in our designated lane, which may have existed only in my American imagination. This frenetic honking and frenzied driving came to define the car rides that took us north of the city to a town whose name, if ever learned, was lost amid the noise and the haste.

Like my school in Guilin these classrooms were full of students both eager to learn English and see a white woman in the flesh for the very first time. And so I taught them and, in turn, they taught me all of the things that I would never have learned if it were not for China.

Around noon, at a hotel near the school, we ate lunch and then laid down to take naps in the darkened rooms of the hotel before returning to the afternoon lesson. These naps came to be my favorite Chinese custom that took place on a daily basis over the course of the school week. But, before we slept, we sat around the table filling the cauldron of broth that stood in the middle of the Lazy Susan with bean curd, bok choy, and mushrooms. Into the mix were thrown pieces of tripe, honeycombed and octagonal, and then these stomachs of ruminating animals were cooked at a rolling boil. At our sides mounds of rice were placed, which we ate with chopsticks, lifting the bowls up to our mouths and slurping all of its contents. Maybe my students were right, maybe I was Chinese after all.

And then something went terribly wrong. The hose that was attached to the propane tank became loose and the flame began to dance too close to the gas line. All of us, all at once, jumped up and scattered from the room leaving only one brave soul behind to turn it off, which he did with the nonchalance of someone who had done this many times before. Soon after, we returned and resumed our meal as if no danger had been adverted, as if nothing happened at all. Perhaps this was indeed the original Chinese fire drill.

At the end of the day, I returned to my apartment in Guilin, forlorn, disoriented, and so much worse for the wear. Once the door was closed, I stripped off my smoke stained clothes and stood underneath the shower until the water ran cold. When darkness enveloped the hills and the sleeping giants returned to their slumber, China grew quiet and I, in turn, grew quiet too. These were the nights that I went to sleep early knowing that all too soon another day would arrive in all of its mayhem and all of its noise, which began long before the rising of the sun.

Most mornings, I was awakened by the truculent noises of Guilin: an old woman calling to collect the garbage, the crow of a rooster, and a man starting his motorcycle on the street below, the engine revving in the darkness as he cleared the phlegm from his. At seven, the morning exercises began. On the field outside, hundreds of students moved in unison to the

163

music that blared on the speakers. As I ate my breakfast of porridge and green tea I'd watch in awe of their uniformity and efficiency. They marched in place, did jumping jacks, and never, not once, stepped out of line. All across China this was how the school day began. Was this the Communism I so feared as a child? It did not seem so awful, but then again, this was only that which was made visible, underneath which lay all that is unheard, unseen, and unspoken.

In the time that we spent together in China, Nina became the best traveling companion that I have ever known. She was (and still is) independent and adventurous, full of life and hunger and a wanton desire to go everywhere and do everything. Needless to say, we probably drove each other crazy as much as we kept one another sane.

Our first trip out of Guilin took us to the Longji Rice Terraces. Built millennia ago, these undulating hills are a veritable topographical map of history chronicling the cultivation of that ancient grain upon which entire civilizations were built. Here, along the backbone of a dragon, we stayed in a *Diaojiaolou*, a suspended guesthouse constructed from bamboo and stones. All along the balconies lanterns and colorful ornate blankets were hung. During the day we walked the cobblestone paths between the rice paddies, exploring the ribs and ridges, as peasants and farmers, wading in the shallow and still water, bent and stooped in order to harvest their crop. Here, women of the Yao minority wore brightly embroidered pink dresses and wrap their hair like turbans around their heads. When twilight cloaked the hills in darkness the moon rose, reflecting a million moons more across the silvered seas and we returned to the lodge to eat quietly from the bounty of their harvest not wishing to wake the now sleeping dragon.

On the weekends that we stayed in Guilin we practiced Chinese with one of Nina's colleagues at her apartment. On Sunday mornings I took a motorbike across town where dogs were seen roasting on the side of the road as families gathered around in anticipation of this feast. Never had I been so happy as to have had eaten breakfast at home that morning.

Upon arrival at Nina's apartment our lesson began and we learned numbers and words, but none proved more useful than the phrase: *Wo bu zhidao,* a phrase necessary in all languages, including your native tongue. It means: I do not know. And it was here, in China, where I first grew comfortable with saying these words aloud.

It was also at Nina's apartment where we celebrated Yom Kippur and Roshashana. In these days of awe, we ate apples covered in honey and atoned for all of our past and future sins. These were the nights that we began our tradition of trying a new fruit every week. Durian was our first curiosity with its protruding spikes and soft flesh. It is the King of Fruits, and if its porcupinian skin was not enough to deter you from eating of its flesh, the smell is said to be its true deterrent. At first I did not know what the big stink was because surely there were things in China that smelled a helluva lot worse than this fruit, but we were able to finish the whole fruit between the two of us. After, we tried mangosteen and rambutan, dragon fruit and lychees, all sweet and full of nectar. Surely, these were the gifts of the gods.

When it was too late for lunch and too early for dinner we ate yams roasted in barrels on the side of the road. They were wrapped in aluminum foil, which kept them warm and sweet. This quickly became our favorite snack, one that reminded Nina of jacket potatoes back home in Birmingham. After we bought two, one for each of us, we found a spot to sit by one of the many lakes of Guilin, peeled away the foil, and sank our teeth into the smoked skin, allowing its sugars to caramelize in our mouths. When we craved something sweeter, we found the men who carved pineapples into succulent sculptures before delivering them to us on bamboo sticks, which we then ate as we walked along the rivers that snaked through the city.

And when we were ravenous we went to one of the many restaurants in Guilin to devour the food that was offered. There was not a week that went by in China that I did not eat the entrails of one animal or another. So as not to offend Nina, who was dissuaded from remaining a carnivore after visiting a slaughterhouse when she was a mere schoolgirl, I explored the corners of the restaurant where meats were displayed. On hooks whole chickens were hung as were the heads and hoofs of pigs, and all of the parts in between and although I might not have always ordered from this bounty, it was a feast for the eyes all the same.

On the nights when we wanted to treat ourselves to something more lavish than our usual fare, we went to the restaurant that served our favorite meal, which was whole snapper with the head still on and the tail firmly intact with the flesh of the fish scored, battered, fried, and then drizzled with a sauce both sour and sweet. The waitress always warned us that this dish took longer to prepare than others, but we both shook our heads as if that motion alone explained that we had already waited our entire lives for a meal such as this.

Of course, this being China, there was also that night where cats were heard in the back room of the restaurant. After ordering my 'chicken', their purr and meows were heard no more. Nina did not have to worry about such things, vegetarian as she was. And still I ate whatever it was that was put in front of me, my Italian mother did not raise me to say no to food.

It was also during our stay in Guilin that a rating system was developed for all of the toilets that we encountered. Nina would not use anything that rated less than a seven. My standards, as always, were a little lower.

After dinner we walked around lakes and rivers of the city, both natural and manmade, pointing out all of the 'ancient' pagodas that had been rebuilt after they had been destroyed during the Cultural Revolution. In the center of the city there was a map of the world painted on the ground below our feet. In the tropical autumn evening Nina and I would stand across from one another, her in England and me in America, shouting across the shallow concrete Atlantic Ocean remembering how far we had come as a waterfall cascaded off the front of a hotel across the way.

When were did not feel like going home just yet we wandered through parks and squares, as monkeys played in the trees and couples waltzed to the orchestras of bamboo flutes and lutes as the fountains danced their water dance. Sometimes a man played an erhu on the sidewalk, running his bow back and forth across the strings of an instrument so full of sorrow that it cast a spell over Guilin and forever enchanted the city and my heart.

As much as I journeyed into the center of the city, there were days that I never left the four walls of my apartment. These were the days that I did not feel brave, I did not dare to be daring, and I certainly was not an adventurer up for an adventure. These were the days that it took all the courage I could muster just to get out of bed.

Do not ever let anyone tell you that all travel is exciting and never once believe that loneliness and anger cannot find you in all the corners of the world, for anger is a shadow, following us wherever we may roam. And my anger, without a ticket, without a passport, without so much as an invitation, followed me all the way to China and it was about time that her and I began to make peace with one another. Thus, my time in China became a sort of self-imposed solitary confinement; a time which was used to grow comfortable with the idea of being uncomfortable, to come to terms with all of my faults and flaws, of which there were many, to learn to be patient and kind in my criticism of myself, to find strength in solitude, and to accept all of my dreams and all of my nightmares as sometimes one in the same.

And this time, more necessary than time spent anywhere else, with anyone else, became all the more precious to me because in my solitude I gave myself permission to be vulnerable and eventually that vulnerability lent itself to humility, then humility offered itself to surrender, and surrender allowed for reckless abandon without which I might have remained forever within the walls of my heart and never found myself beyond its limits, for sometimes, it is only by traveling beyond our zones of comfort that we are able to reach so deeply within ourselves so that we may live fully the depth and breadth of our existence.

Small wonder that the Chinese call their land Zhongguo, meaning the Middle Kingdom, more often referred to as the center of the universe. This, too, was a journey to my center.

Although there were days when the idea of being a hermit was oh so appealing, there were also days in China when this solitude had no place in my life. While in China email proved to be one of the best and newest of modern technological advances that made it easier to stay in touch with friends and family back home and I tried to stay in touch with them all.

The summer before I left for China I coached lacrosse for a Long Island travel team. The girls were rising juniors, soon to end their high school tenure and then set off to set the world on fire. Only five years older than they, I kept in contact with some of the girls from the team and we wrote back and forth about all the things that were important to us; them telling me of the adventures they were having applying to college and me telling them the adventures I was having half a world away. One of my favorite players was a girl named Ali, who was-and probably still is-one of the funniest people that I have ever met. One fateful night, this was the email that was received from Ali:

Your mission, should you choose to accept it, is to find Chinese break-dancers and become friends with them.

This message will self-destruct in five seconds.

It seemed like a mission damn near impossible, so half joking, half serious, I promised her that I would try my best. After all, the purpose of life is to believe in impossibilities just as much as possibilities.

And so that night, as was our Friday tradition, Nina and I went to dinner at one of our favorite restaurants where we ate string beans sautéed with ginger and scallions, sweet potato cakes, and rice, always rice. As we parted ways and made plans for the rest of the weekend there they were, b-boys break dancing in the night. Some wore loose jeans and backwards hats. Others had bleached blond hair and fresh low tops. In the center square they listened to Chinese rap and American hip hop as they wind milled, popped and locked, and spun on their heads. I closed my eyes, half hoping that it was just a dream because it seemed as if I had finally lost my mind after spending too much time alone and not enough time with the world at large, but when I opened them again, there they were doing the snake, doing the freak, doing the whop.

I sat on the edge of a bench dumbfounded by what I had just encountered. Were they for real? Of course they were. That these things actually happen shows that the universe is not only listening, but that it also has a sense of humor. I sat there long enough for one of them to come over, curious as to not only why a white woman was in their city, but also why she was watching them as intently as she was. Although he was no more fluent in English than I was in Chinese, a fast friendship was formed. After all, it is difficult not to be friends with someone whose very few phrases in the English language included *"What's going on?"* and *"Fucking bullshit!"*

I could not wait to go home and tell Ali that her mission had been accomplished, but not before exchanging numbers with Tang Yi and saying goodbye to all of my newfound friends.

At first Tang Yi invited me to their battles and then he invited me to his home to have dinner with his family, which I willingly obliged to because there are few better ways to learn about a person or a culture than sharing a meal. When I found myself at Tang Yi's doorstep, he welcomed me inside and gave me a tour of the apartment that he shared with his family. After the tour was complete he unrolled a watercolor of a pastoral landscape, a palimpsest painted upon the pages of the newspaper. Here, a

170

river ran through the village and two figures, a son and a father, crossed a footbridge and a small fishing boat moored along the bank. It was beautiful in its simplicity and proved that not only was Tang Yi a break-dancer, he was also an artist.

In the kitchen, a room with a concrete floor, a gas stove, and a small water basin, his mother asked if I would help her to cook this meal. Together, we grated ginger, scored scallions, and broke soft tofu in our fingers before wrapping all of these ingredients in the dough that she had prepared before my arrival. Since neither of us spoke the language of the other we mimed our intentions and settled into the syncopated silence of wrapping each dumpling and sealing the wanton with our fingers. Some of these dumplings were dropped in oil and we watched as they sizzled and tanned in the pan and their edges curl from the heat. The rest were steamed, growing softer and glistening all the more as they were removed from the water. When we finished cooking we sat on tiny step stools around the plate in the center. There was no table. Only this. In Chinese culture it is rude to refuse both food and drink. But because these dumplings were so unbelievably delicious, it was impossible not to say no to more. I ate so many I almost burst (and to this day, they are still the best darn dumplings I have ever had). When I left, Tang Yi rolled up his painting and gave it to me with a smile that never seemed to leave his face and from that day, wherever I have lived, this painting, painted by a Chinese break-dancer, has hung on the wall of my bedroom in its bamboo frame.

Four full moons came and went and soon it was December. This year was to be my first Christmas away from my family. In Guilin, men dressed up as Santa Claus with their red hats, black boots, white trim beards, and, for some inexplicable reason, braided pigtails on either side, which actually made their costume all the more festive and made the distance between China and New York all the less.

So as to celebrate the holidays, I flew to Beijing where I met a British lad by the name of Simon who was as fond of walking as he was of American fast food. Together we climbed the Great Wall, not the popular tourist section, no, we were much too good for that, but a stretch of the wall where the effects of time were apparent in the crumbling stones and falling ramparts. It was only there, along this small section of wall, that I finally learned that the Great Wall, contrary to my naïve belief, was not a gently sloping wall that separated China from its invaders to the North (and from wherever else they came), but a mountain, a valley, a river, and a dragon upon which there seemed to be no beginning and no end. And as we walked from tower to tower, I thought to myself how strange it was that sometimes the walls that are built to keep people out are the very same walls that can also imprison us, or, at the very least, keep us from the rest of the world.

After, we entered the Forbidden City, we grew quiet in Tiananmen Square, and we visited the Summer Palace in the middle of winter. For dinner we ate Peking duck and dared one another to try all of the impaled insects found on bamboo skewers in the food stalls of the night market. In Hutong we celebrated New Year's Eve, but this was the Gregorian calendar and the real New Year, the Chinese New Year, was yet to come.

As always happens with people you meet while traveling, we soon parted ways, he back to England and I to all of the places where my heart longed to be; the places full of history and mystery.

On my return from Beijing, I explored the former home of Chiang

Hai Chek and Madame Chiang Hai Chek, the Jinsha River, and the Longmen Grottoes where for miles on end Buddha's large and small are carved into the bedrock thousands of years before creating both a mountain of sculptures and sculptures in mountains.

My final and perhaps most important stop on the way back to Guilin was to visit the monks of Shaolin. There I found them clad as they were in their saffron robes practicing impossible feats of acrobatics. It would be a bold faced lie if I had said that I went to Shaolin because of my lifelong interest in Chinese martial arts. The real reason was not my love of Bruce Lee or Kung Fu, but because of a youth spent listening to RZA, GZA, and the rest of the Wu Tang Clan. It must be noted that I did not need to travel halfway around the world to go their Shaolin, for I had already been there, but China and Staten Island are not the same at all. There I stayed only for an afternoon, or about the time that it takes to pass through Staten Island during rush hour before returning to Guilin once more.

The cold that arrived with January no longer allowed the concrete walls of my apartment to hold the heat they once did and on the other side of the equator there was Australia where it was still summer, where it was still warm. Faced with the choice of staying or leaving, I chose to depart because the opportunity to coach lacrosse and see about a boy were both too tempting to resist.

And so, before travelling to another hemisphere, Nina and I embarked on one last journey to see all the places that we still had yet to see and all of the places we may never see again. We began in the Stone Forest of Shilin where we stood dwarfed by stalagmites said to be over two hundred and seventy million years old. At the bottom of an impenetrable sea of petrified trees that towered above our heads, never had I felt so small, so insignificant, so impermanent. For hours we wandered in silence through this maze carved by retreating waters, lost in the beauty of China for which there are no words.

After we visited pandas in a bamboo forest. At the Giant Buddha of Leshan, we climbed down from his head to his toes and back up again. The Buddha smiled as we passed, an unwavering and all knowing smirk that he has smirked for the last twelve hundred years. We walked along the narrow streets of Lijiang, where there were no cars, only water mills that slowly spun outside of homes covered with terra cotta tiles and villagers that passed by with their pushcarts and milkmaid's yokes around their shoulders. Here it was as if time stood still and if it were not for the electricity that lit the cobblestone streets at night it would have been difficult to prove that the year was now 2004. This was all the China of my imagination; cities suspended in time, black and white animals feasting on leaves from bamboo trees, indomitable landscapes, and Buddha's in solemn stillness. If I had only traveled to China to see this, it would have been worth it all.

At a restaurant in Lijiang we came across a group of Americans, young adventurers ready to climb mountains, or, at the very least, the mountain that rose like the moon over this city. Without question I joined them for their escapade and in the morning we ascended into the valley between the mountains of the Jade Dragon Snow and Haba Xueshan by means of the twenty-eight bends. As we hiked along the gorge, steep and wild, a chill rose in the air, cold enough to freeze the small waterfalls that ran down the crags and into the river, which was at first wide and calm, and then began to rage below us. Somewhere along the edge of the ravine we were told the story of how this place came to be named the Tiger Leaping

Gorge. As legend has it:

Once there was a hunter who chased a tiger through the valley and into the most narrow of chasms. The hunter, unwilling to give up, closed in on the tiger just where the gorge is the most precarious and the most perilous. But the tiger, forever courageous and brave, listening to *l'appel du vide*, leapt across the gorge and risked his tiger life to escape from certain death and it is said that if you look closely you can still see the marks of his claws on the rocks on the other side.

As I looked across the river to find truth in this tale I thought how it is that some days we are the hunter and some days we are the hunted and when we arrive at the places where we are asked to either stay or leave, we leap, we pause, we pause, we leap, forever torn between roots and wings.

When the winter sun disappeared behind the mountains, we made our way to the hostel to warm our souls with the sweet breads of naxi baba and to warm our bones with that drink of life: green tea. When this meal was finished and our bellies were full we left the artificial light of our hostel, which was only a few lanterns and loose light bulbs strung around the room, and stepped into a world without electricity. In the great expanse of the mountains and the empyrean, constellations, more than all the myths in the world, filled the cold and cloudless sky and danced above the snow capped peaks as we stood in silence and awe upon the ground below.

When the rest of the world was sleeping, I found my way to the 'toilet,' which was really only a trough carved into the rocks, open to all of the elements of heaven and earth. In the stillness, I crouched low to the stones attempting to stay as underexposed as possible as the wind howled its winter song and looked out again into the space between terra firma and the firmament, and I realized that here, in this place, in this moment, I was witnessing the collapsing and unfolding of the universe and for the shortest
175

of moments there was no loneliness, there was no void. For that moment, it had been filled. Even after I returned to bed my mind still saw stars and that night I learned just how difficult it is to sleep when you are that close to heaven.

The next morning, we descended the mountain just in time to rejoice in the Chinese New Year. As the darkness of the new moon enveloped Dali, the light from fireworks flooded the streets as dragons danced and drums beat on. It was no small coincidence that I travelled to China in the Year of the Monkey. I, too, was born in the year of the Monkey and there is no more perfect way to end a journey to China than to come full circle and begin anew and from Kunming I flew to Hong Kong and then onto Melbourne, Australia.

For years after I was haunted by memories of China. The smell of a street, the carving of a pineapple, the blaring of a car horn, the waning and waxing of the moon, all brought me back to a place unparalleled and never to be repeated. China, for me, will forever occupy that space between all that is real and all that is imagined. China will always be my ghost.

Perhaps it is because China was so foreign, so expansive, so unfamiliar from anything I had ever known that it created an earthquake in my soul, the magnitude of which was not measured at the time, but only afterwards, with tremors and aftershocks arriving in waves of repercussive awe; an awe that still permeates my entire being and sinks into my soul only to be reawakened and remembered in times when needed most.

For this is what traveling, the best kind of traveling does: It surprises us. It disorients, confounds, and bewilders us so that, if we are lucky, we are never, ever the same.

And if ever life, that sly, sly thief, were to steal my memories from me, one by one, I hope that these memories are among the last to be taken.

On Australia

I blame everything on Paris. I blame it on Claude Monet and Ernest Hemingway, I blame it on the Seine, I blame it on mousse au chocolat, and I blame it on champagne. Most of all I blame it on a universe that believes in both chaos and destiny, which are often one and the same. Had it not been for Paris, there would never have been Oscar, and had it not been for Oscar there would never have been Oliver. So therefore, it is the fault of France and not my own.

The transition from East to West was as sudden as it was slow. What a strange sensation it was to be surrounded by English speakers once again and even stranger to be an American at a time when America was drawing such harsh criticism from both its allies and its enemies. This made it all the more difficult to be a diplomat, reluctant patriot as I was, and both attempt to defend and deny a country that was so very far away.

In Melbourne, I was to coach lacrosse. Less than two years out of college and I missed the game, but really I missed a past that can never be repeated no matter how often it is returned to through coaching and not playing and so it was in Australia that I learned that a coach I am not since I prefer to be on the field rather than on the sidelines.

If I was to be honest, I went to Australia not for lacrosse, but because Oscar lived there and I was curious, silly woman that I am, to see if he was perhaps one of the greats, one of the three loves that Sonny told Calogero about in *A Bronx Tale*, which of course, he wasn't, but there would be less 'fun' to this story if that was the case and besides, to this day, I have yet to shake the hopeless romanticism that has both contoured and corrupted my heart.

At the end of January, I arrived in Melbourne to see about the fates, but when I stayed with Oscar, I felt as an intruder must feel when they are caught in all of the places they are not supposed to be. By then, too much time had passed. We were not in Europe anymore. Still a Gentile, I was severely out of place and realized all too suddenly that there are things that have no place in the present and therefore should be left in the past only to be revisited in our memories and nowhere else. One thing that I should have learned by then, but did not because I am bull headed and slow to learn when it comes to matters of the heart, was that there are no lessons to be learned from chasing after boys, except for one:

DO NOT CHASE AFTER BOYS.

Less than two weeks later, I left his house and moved into a house on Bambra Road, where I shared a room with Daniel, a mulatto football player from England. In our separate beds we binged watched reality television and munched on Crunchies before we fell asleep and every morning he woke up, rubbed his eyes, and said, "*Fuckin 'el*," in his Cockney accent as he yawned and stretched away the night. In this house there was also Renata, a young girl from Germany who taught me how to say "*Vas ees das?"* in German of course, and as we ate our breakfasts together I obnoxiously asked her over and over again: *"What is this?"* in German, always in German. To round out our motley crew there were also two couples, one pair hailing from Ireland and the other from the United Kingdom. Together, we lived in Caulfield for months and at the end of our collective sojourn, we rented a car and road tripped it along the Great Ocean Road where we saw koalas and kangaroos, and wallabies. We passed the Twelve Apostles on our way to Bell's Beach where there was no fifty-year storm of which to speak, only the sun and the sand and the waves and the sea.

By April, as the Antarctic currents shifted cooling the air and ushering in autumn; it was time to move on. As the days grew colder and shorter I was told to head north along the coast to Byron Bay, for there, it was still summer, at least for a little while longer. Had I know then, as I packed all of my belongings, that I was on a collision course with fate from which there was no turning back, I might have stayed, I might not have gone, but life unfolds as it should and as it must and so I bought a one-way ticket to New South Wales.

At first light the bus pulled off the Pacific Highway. Here along the eastern most point of Australia, before Captain James Cook named this northeastern corner of New South Wales after "Foul Weather Jack", John Byron, the local Arakwal Aboriginal people referred to this region as *Cavvanbah*, meaning; "meeting place." This, too, was where I was to meet with my Morai.

The hostel was a short walk from the bus station and only one hundred meters from the beach, which of course was the first place I went before ever dropping off my bags. Walking upon white sand that squished and squeaked between my toes and looking out across the enormity of the Pacific Ocean I thought to myself: Yes, this is where I will empty my

183

pockets and fill the rest of my days.

There a shipwreck lay just off the shores; its mast still visible above the shoals where the waves break clean and warm. At the invitation of the ocean I surfed on a board not meant for beginners ever wondering why I could not stand up no matter how perfect the wave. And yet, being out there in the water, day in and day out, no matter how awful of a surfer I might have been, was the one of the most magnificent times of my life. Here, I did not need to be anywhere else and I most certainly did not need to be anyone else. All that was asked was to paddle out into the water and surrender to the sea.

At eventide, when the sun sank over Australia and the moon waxed over the ocean blue, I almost did not notice the fin rising out of the water and its all too menacing shadow lurking below, but when I did, I stopped breathing, lifted my arms and legs out of the water, and turned my board towards the shore. A moment later, another fin emerged from the water less than ten feet away and for the first time in a long time I was scared. Just as I began to make peace with death or dismemberment, the porpoises, not sharks, began to play among the waves, jumping in and out of the water and after what seemed an eternity I finally exhaled. The day was gone. They night had begun.

And then I met him. He sat at the top of the steps with a sketchpad on his lap and a pencil worn down to its eraser between his fingers. From his lips hung a hand rolled cigarette from which he occasionally took drags without ever using his hands. A book lay open to his side. It was *Papillion,* the story of a French criminal forever attempting to escape from prison. Had

I read this book before meeting him maybe I would have understood more, and maybe I would have fought less, but until then I had never heard of Henri Charriere or Devil's Island, so the meaning of its pages were lost to the night.

Curious as to who he was and what he was doing so very far away from the place where he called home, I sat by his side and learned that he was a carpenter and a surfer and that he was here about a girl whose heart he had broken and hoped to mend. Hearing only the first part and blatantly ignoring the second, it was then that I began to pay attention to his sun kissed skin and his brown brown eyes that did nothing to hide his mischievous spirit, they only revealed it. His name was Oliver and he was from South Africa. He spoke with an accent, lacing his English with Afrikaans words like *bru, boet, and hoezit.* So, of course I fell in love with him right then and there. I had no other choice. Allowing my hopeless romanticism to get the best of me once again- such a silly silly girl- I called Lauren the next day to tell her that I met the man I was going to marry and like the best of friends, she believed me as if these words, once spoken, must always become the truth.

In the afternoons, after he had finished work for the day, he would come find me and say: "*Come on you short shit, we're going to surfing.*" And off we went in his combie with our boards on the roof and the windows rolled down, but we never left the parking lot until listening to "Fall Line" by Jack Johnson over and over again. On our way back, salt skinned and sun drunk, we listened to it once more, never tiring of this one minute and thirty-four second song.

Before night fell I ran to the lighthouse that stood at the tip of the town to say goodbye to the day, sometimes alone, sometimes with Sasha, another traveller from Germany also intent on finding his way. Most days,

185

we raced to the top and when we reached the summit, we stood at edge of the world and faced east towards the great expanse of the Pacific, somewhere beyond which lay America and I longed for my land and for my people once more.

As summer slipped ever so casually into fall we sat drinking beers and cheap wine around the campfire. There were many of us, but I always found myself next to Oliver. In the light of the dancing flames we told each other jokes as he rolled cigarettes between his fingers, licking its edges before placing it between his pursed lips. We sat close, but not too close, and yet for me it was never close enough. By then I was a goner, a girl foolish enough to believe in soul mates and love at first sight and all of the things that make this life both sour and sweet. If I had known then how easy it is to fall in love and how difficult it is to keep love aflame, perhaps then I would have exercised more caution, but where would the fun be in knowing things like that?

By the middle of May, the yearning returned, not to travel to distant places, but to the place closest to my heart. Ten months had passed. Almost three hundred days. It was time to go home.

On the day of departure, Oliver drove me to Brisbane. Before we got in the car, we walked on the beach for one last memory. There, he picked up small shells and gave them to me so that I remember Byron Bay, so that I might remember him; how little he realized how impossible he would be to forget. When he dropped me off at the airport I asked him to come to New York one day to find me. It didn't matter when, he just had to come find me so that I might know what it was like to kiss him, to love him, and maybe even marry him. And then we said goodbye.

On Shattered Dreams

On the 4th of June 2004, I returned to New York to surprise my mother on her fifty-fourth birthday. As always, the whole of the family was there to share in her revelry and it was a joy to be among their ranks once again.

When I first saw Matty, he had to have known where I had been and why I was there, after all, I came back with boxes of chocolate covered macadamia nuts and stories half told, but he never said anything and neither did I. How could I when he had just been diagnosed with lung cancer, a cancer that was in its final stage, and had already metastasized in his intestines? In other words, how could I when my grandfather was dying?

On the day after Christmas a tsunami fell upon Asia. What began as an earthquake at the bottom of the sea swelled to the surface and brought devastation to the shores of the surrounding landmasses and hundreds of thousands of lives were lost and like the waters that recede and then flood, I watched as his health declined, retreating only to destroy. Maybe it was that Matty, whose disease claimed his lungs, the place where grief is kept, was suffocating in his own sadness. Maybe it was not the war that he still fought after 1945. Maybe it was only himself. Sometimes war and fate share the same casualties and the same cruelties.

In between rounds of chemotherapy and radiation there was never time to tell him what a good man his son is and what a beautiful family he has and what a beautiful life he lives. I did not get a chance to tell him that his son has his eyes, that his son had his patience, or lack thereof, and that sometimes his son sang Hawaiian songs and smiled for no reason at all. And my grandfather would never know that even though he grew up on Oahu and not in Brooklyn, his son still spoke like him, walked like him, and acted like him; as if time and distance could not erase these paternal tendencies passed from father to son.

But there was never a time to tell him how much my Uncle John reminded me of him and there was never time to tell him that his son still loved him even though they never met. There was never a time to tell him any of these things because the cancer that grew in his lungs and spread throughout his body stripped him of his strength and whatever hair that remained on his head. Besides, would it have eased his pain or simply caused him to suffer more?

As he lay dying on his hospital bed with tubes that ran the length of his body, pumping air into his lungs because they could no longer do so themselves, he looked at me, his eyes searching my own for forgiveness that was not mine to give, but I offered it nevertheless. One last breath and then he was gone.

After we buried my grandfather in the frozen ground of February, death became a near constant companion for my family. In the months that followed a generation was lost: Sisters. Brothers. Aunts. Uncles. Cousins. Even the Great Aunt Fannie. Seven in total; one for almost every month of the year. For twelve months our family reunions took place in funeral homes across the Island and Brooklyn between the hours of two to five and seven to ten.

Death is funny that way.

He brings people together just as much as he rents them apart.

In February, just weeks after my grandfather died, when the ground was still covered in ice and snow, Oliver came. He had come all the way from Australia, really he arrived via London, but there is no sense in introducing romance to a story if you do not allow yourself an exaggeration here or there.

Ready to introduce him to all food New York: pizza and cannolis, coffee and bagels, we drove down Main Street into the village of Northport, an hour east of the city. Once there he asked: "*Where are all the big buildings?*" As if all of New York is Manhattan. In the frigid cold we walked on the dock where there were no boats in the harbor, just a setting sun across the bay. We leaned into one another, as old friends do after a long separation, but my heart knew that friends we were not long to stay.

Oliver's visit lasted for only one week and when he left I longed for him in a way that I had never felt before and may never again and the place where he resided in my heart was full in his presence, yet empty in his absence. Perhaps it is only now that I realize that I loved Oliver the way only the young are able to love: fearlessly, recklessly, hopelessly, and desperately.

After, Oliver became my reason to escape New York every chance I got and over the course of our transcontinental love affair I flew to London every other month. Who the fuck did I think I was? Oh, that's right, I was young, stupid, and in love with a disposable income, which in hindsight, should have been put to better use, with a passport whose pages screamed to be filled, and nothing more than time on her hands. Would I do it again? Without a doubt.

April arrived, but my period did not arrive with it. It was late. It was never late. At the pharmacy, I bought all of the pregnancy tests on the shelf and took one after another, all revealing what my body already knew, but my brain refused to acknowledge: I was pregnant. That night, in Addie's arms, I cried, weeping uncontrollably for things that could and should have been prevented. I was petrified and ashamed, scared and embarrassed. In two months I was to leave for the Peace Corps. I could not have a child, not now, and possibly not ever.

Sometime after midnight a decision was made quickly, but not lightly. There were things to consider. At that age, at that moment, I knew that I could not provide the life that this child deserved, a life that I might never be able to offer. Old fears of loss and abandonment that had been sown into my soul as a child resurfaced. And a newer, more selfish fear arose, a fear that this child might turn out just like me: full of fury and rage and heat and passion, readily willing and able to tell her parents that she hated them and did not need anyone because it is safer to be alone than to be surrounded by anyone else. I do not think that my heart could have handled a daughter such as me and I do not know how my mother's did. It was for these reasons that I never told my mother of my pregnancy; afraid that she might ask me to keep something that could not be kept, afraid that she might hate me for my decision so final, so absolute.

Just as the sun began to cast away the shadows of the night I called Oliver. He remained quiet, unwilling to ask the questions that weighed heavily on both of our hearts: Were we not careful? Were we that reckless? Did we not know better? After the phone was hung up an appointment was made for the Wednesday of the following week.

In the morning the sun hid behind clouds that promised rain and nothing else. Outside of the gates to Planned Parenthood a small group of people were gathered to protest the choice that wa. They carried signs speaking of psalms and shouted an by and I wondered if they had ever looked into their o much intensity as the light they now shined on me.

My sister Michele, who was driving, turned into th away from the antipathetic crowd. Then it began to rain. l ...ue my name was called and I was brought into a small room without windows where all was white and sterile and blinding in the artificial light. Once disrobed, the nurse covered my mouth and nose and asked me to count backwards from ten, nine, eight…

Hours later I woke up on Kristen's couch, sore and disoriented, wondering why it was that Oliver had not called. And still it rained.

After, I don't remember wanting the same things anymore…

Just two days later I boarded a plane to London. Outside of customs, he pulled me in close without saying a word. His hands were warm and damp like they always were after too long apart. In silence we drove back to a hotel where we were to stay as I recovered. Once there, I drew myself a bath and as the steam rose from the surface, I sank into the water below. In the hot liquid that scorched and scolded my body, I wanted to scream, I wanted to cry, I wanted to be ashamed of my decision, but I did not feel any of those things. I was numb.

Late in the morning we walked along the Thames, silently waiting for spring to arrive, but we did not speak of anything, not even this. We never spoke of this. And as boats went up and down the river, back and forth went my thoughts between what silence there is in shame and what shame there is in silence.

193

later I do not remember whose pain was greater, his, or mine as if as a competition, as if losing suddenly became more important than winning and that somehow the greater the loss, the greater the victory.

Even memories have their cold spots, haunted as they are by the ghosts of our mistakes and our regrets.

Even now, with the clarity of hindsight, I find it difficult to write about something that I do not understand and may never understand. In all honesty, I will fail. I will fall short. But I will do my best not to assign guilt where there is none or point fingers in directions they do not belong. I will write only as I remember. Then, in my youth meant only for mistakes and misunderstandings, I had yet to take up residence in the House of Gathering and it was difficult to understand all that was to happen next when I was still boxing with my own shadow.

Caught in the throes of Youthful American Idealism, I applied to the Peace Corps. In the hope of volunteering in Central or South America, I learned Spanish, but fate, that fickle beast, would not have it that way. Instead, she sent me to Jamaica, a country in which Spanish is not spoken, but still, a country that I all too readily agreed to go.

In the weeks prior to my departure Damien Marley's *Welcome to Jamrock* played on the radio. It began: "*Out on the streets they call it murder.*" While it is true that, in July of 2005, Jamaica had the highest murder rate in the world, that song was the most harsh, albeit realistic, way to be introduced to a place. But then again what peace was I to bring to Jamaica when there was no peace to be found within me?

After arriving on this Caribbean island, it was apparent that this Jamaica was very different from the Jamaica of the all-inclusive resorts that rimmed its perimeter, which was perfectly fine with me because I was neither there as a tourist nor was I there for vacation. Far from. Because of my construction experience, I was assigned to the Water Sanitation committee, which I knew absolutely nothing about, but hey, I was here to learn, right? And so, in the equatorial heat I shaved my head down to a quarter of an inch, because it was so much better to cut it all off than waste the water I was there to conserve.

As part of our training we stayed in Heartease, a small town east of Kingston. There we lived with Jamaican families so as to learn patois and Caribbean culture. In the mornings, the heat that not even night could temper rose ever higher and even in the early hours of the day the air stood thick and windstill under the burning and blazing sun. After training the volunteers who lived in the neighborhood walked home together, sometimes stopping for a Red Stripe at one of cabarets along the way. On wooden stools in front of wooden counters we spoke to one another about our dreams and all that we hoped to accomplish while we were here and we spoke with the Jamaicans who called Heartease their home and they shared the stories of their lives with us and introduced us to their children, their food, and their music and at night, those tropical nights, this music rose in the darkness enveloping the island in rhythm and bass.

In the last days of our training those of us who were to work with the Department of Sanitation were taken to the place just outside of Kingston where the garbage from the entire island was collected. On a one-lane road, littered with refuses and mud, shacks were raised with corrugated roofs and tarpaulin doors and the stray wires, which were wrapped around makeshift antennas, provided electricity for those that resided within while outside wild pigs scavenged for food among the muck.

When we entered the complex, men carrying Kalashnikovs rifles escorted us through the facility. Who were they protecting us from? And what peace was ever accomplished at the end of a rifle?

196

After our grand tour of the facilities another volunteer and I, both light of skin, boarded a bus back to Kingston. As we drove through Trenchtown, along streets of broken pavement and rusted zinc, the woman behind us on the crowded bus clutched her bag tightly to her bosom and made the sign of the cross. After she said her prayers she muttered something about the two of us being crazy white people who had no business being where we were under her breath. Whether she intended for the two of us to hear her does not matter because crime and violence and war do not differentiate among skin colors and what happens to one can happen to all. What did matter in that moment was that a reality was born in me that I had never experienced before; a reality that told of people who live with these fears and still found the courage not only to survive, but to thrive. This instant opened my eyes to a world I had never known, but once known could never be forgotten or ignored. And while I now understood the impossibility of closing my eyes after this experience, it was my heart that had not opened just yet.

By August, I stood on a precipice. If I fell on which side would I land? Would it hurt? We balance along the edge between holding on and letting go. We can never do both. We can only choose one. With these questions dancing around in my head I called Oliver in South Africa and said: *"I can stay here in Jamaica and keep chasing this dream- even though my dream is a little different now- or I can leave and be with you."* (What I was really saying was "I can chase you." Silly woman, how long would it take for me to learn this lesson?) Had I listened to the part of my heart that was supposed to love myself first and foremost I would have requested a transfer from Jamaica and followed through living this dream, but silly me, I listened to the part of my heart that still believed we are allowed only one great love in our lives and no more. Believing only this I chose Oliver.

But still it was that five weeks was all that it took to realize that Jamaica was not where I wanted to be. Perhaps I had fallen victim of the Peace Corps way of weeding people out. And so I quit the Peace Corps, partly because I had been told that projects, once begun, if ever begun at all, might never see completion, but mostly because, only two months later, I was still healing emotionally and physically from my abortion.

On my last night in Jamaica I sat among the hills overlooking Kingston and glanced out into a country I would never know, all the while thinking how delicate dreams are, how easily they shatter. The next morning I was on a plane back to New York.

By then, my grandmother was sleeping in my room. Without a bed, I slept on the couch in our den, while my mother, in constant fear of her mother falling, placed a bell on Connie's night table, which she asked my grandmother to ring if ever she needed anything.

That summer my grandmother was singlehandedly responsible for giving all of the angels their wings.

When the summer ended, Oliver returned to London from South Africa, where he had gone to visit his family. We had not seen one another since July, since before the Peace Corps. For weeks there had been distance between us, as if an ocean and a continent were not enough and rather than breaching the distance between us, we grew further apart.

At the end of the month I flew to England. As always, he picked me up at the airport and we rode the tube back to the apartment that he shared with his best friend, Kyle. When everyone else had fallen asleep, he shared with me of a story that was told to him while he was in South Africa that forever changed the way Oliver saw the world and his place in it and together we wept.

In London, I could not stay so I spent what little money I had and flew to Florence to stay with Rosa and Francesco, for Florence was the only place where I hoped that I could grow to understand what might never be understood. There, I spent too many days smoking cigarettes on the edge of the Arno and too many nights crying myself to sleep over unchangeable pasts and unpredictable futures.

On my last night in Italy, we went to a restaurant in a town that overlooked all of Tuscany. Below, Brunelleschi's dome was cloaked in the fading light as the bells of the Campanile rang out across the city. There, we drank red wine from glasses without stems and we ordered *Bistecca Florentina,* served rare with the blood still oozing from the flesh of the beef. As we ate they shared the stories of their lives, their loves, and their heartbreaks. When I told them of the reasons why the 'love of my life' was no longer in my life my uncle told me that some problems are just too big. Always a stubborn and irrational creature and unable to separate my head from my heart, I did not listen. In hindsight, I should have listened to Francesco, but love had not only made me blind, it has also made me deaf and I temporarily lived in fear of hearing the truth: that not all loves are meant to last forever.

I returned to New York with nothing but a broken heart.

Throughout October, I spent my days with my grandmother, Concetta, trying to make her laugh, but laughter for either of us did not come easily. Instead, she stared out the window as the earth tilted away from the sun and said only three words, words spoken thousands of times since she lost her husband: "*I miss Matty*," as if the more she said these words the more likely he was to come back, but he never did. In the days, weeks, and months to come my grandmother and I were put on strict rules on how many times a day we were allowed to mention our lost loves; rules that we happily broke, if only between one another.

By the end of October, I had called Oliver too many times. Refusing to let go, I held on too tight. If there was a difference between support and suffocation, I had yet to learn it. But then again, eternal optimist that I am I still believed that love, and only love, was enough. But sometimes love does not conquer all. Sometimes love only conquers and after a while, he stopped taking my phone calls.

Somewhere between Thanksgiving and Christmas he called to say that he missed me, that he loved me still, and that he wanted to get back together. Had I been a little less weak of will I would have taken longer to consider his proposition, but love had made me a fool and for Christmas I bought a plane ticket bound for South Africa and in the New Year off I went to Oliver with my broken heart convinced that I could love him enough for the both of us.

I arrived at night, always at night. At the airport he stood on the other side of the glass with his hands in his pockets and a smile on his face and I was a goner once again.

When the sun had arched across the southern tip of Africa, I glimpsed Table Mountain for the first time. In the near distance clouds blanketed and rolled across the flattened top, descending down the mountain like a river of fog and mist. It was unsurprising how easy it was to be swept away by the romanticism of it all after years spent reading Ernest Hemingway and Kuki Gallman and aching for the day when my feet finally found this land of dust and earth, a place where there were elephants and lions, giraffes and zebras, baboons and even sharks, but, most of all, this was where Oliver was. As night fell, we went to his local to drink sundowners as we watched and waited for that flash of green, that last spark of light before the sun was swallowed by the sea.

That first Sunday the boys: Oliver, his brothers, and all of their friends, prepared a braai. Over open coals went the boerewors, sosaties, and snoek. When we sat down to eat they spoke of all of their youthful (mis)adventures in Kruger National Park where they were awakened in the night by hyenas; their eyes and teeth gleaming in the darkness, their stench permeating the air. They told stories of what it was like to drive through the Karoo, fearful that they might run out of petrol and of their days spent surfing in the frigid waters off the coast, sharing the sea with great white sharks. After whiskey their tales grew darker and they began to speak of their lives both during and after Apartheid. They spoke of their fears and frustrations, of beauty and tragedy, of violence and an unbeknownst peace and the reality they had known lay in stark contrast with my own.

And yet here, which was once named *Cabo das Tormentas (Cape of Storms,)* but now is called the Cape of Good Hope, I refused to believe that all was lost. After all, it had only been eleven years since the end of

201

Apartheid and change, real change, is slow, often going unseen in one lifetime.

For holiday, we drove along the Western Cape. On the hills of the Garden Route he pointed out the wildlife: "*Look, babe! Brazilian Water Buffalo!*" Expecting to see wild beasts, I looked and sure enough, there they were, cows grazing on the side of a hill, or as Oliver called it, in the softness of his South African accent where he traded all of his h's for y's, a *yill*.

When we arrived at the game reserve, impala and kudu ran across the plains as elephants swayed and swung their trunks from side to side and giraffes stretched and craned their necks towards the sky. Before supper, in the quiet of the South African twilight, we drank glasses of sherry and watched a rhinoceros wade into a shallow watering hole and a lone zebra graze on the high grasses. Somewhere, a lion roared and I knew that this moment, this place, this man, was all that I ever wanted.

Two weeks had passed, but they were not enough, so back to South Africa I went, this time to live. The days between my return and departure were spent with my grandmother. In the early spring we went for rides in my 1989 Ford F150, pale green and rusted from the road and the relentless rush of time. Most days I helped her climb into the cab, for the lift was too high and her body was too small. She laughed as we drove down the streets, me shifting from second to third and her tumbling and bouncing in the passenger seat even though we both knew that the smile on her face did little to hide her sorrow.

It had only been little over a year since Matty died, since Connie grandmother lost her sweetheart. And so it was that on Fat Tuesday, when my mother asked her mother what it was she was going to give up for Lent, she replied: *"My life."* Sometime after Easter, after He had risen, she had fallen. She broke her hip. But it was not to my parent's house that she returned to after she left the hospital. Instead, she was taken to hospice, where she descended into her long night as April showers fell outside.

That was the day that we learned that it is indeed possible to die of a broken heart.

Unable to change my ticket of departure, I left my mother without her mother. I left the States in the middle of my grandmother's wake and before her funeral. I left because it was too difficult to imagine my life without my mother and it was impossible to watch as my mother mourned her own.

That year, had death not taken enough?

In South Africa, the winds shifted again and summer was no more. In the mornings, after Oliver left for work, I ran along the Western Cape, climbing the small hills that rose up between the two oceans. As one hill crested into another I was confronted with an unadulterated view of Robben Island, the place where Nelson Mandela spent twenty-seven years of his life; a year longer than my lifetime. There, as the sun, almost at its apex, cast its light and not its darkness across the water, I was reminded that not all of us are born free, some of us, most of us, must fight for our freedoms, and that to experience just one day of freedom, real freedom, might actually be worth a lifetime of imprisonment.

But in South Africa I could not stay, for in Blouberg, along the blue mountain beach, we lived with Oliver's roommate and his roommate's girlfriend. Under one roof, the four of us slept with all of our angels and even more of our demons. This type of living situation would be taxing on even the most stable of relationships and here Oliver and I were still trying to build ours upon solid ground.

And so I left, AGAIN, and he arrived in America not too long after. It was the middle of September when he came to stay and an apartment was rented down the street from the beach complete with a fenced in porch, a fireplace, and ten foot ceilings. At night, after Oliver returned from work, we ate dinner and played chess. Sometimes I won, sometimes I lost. Sometimes he won, sometimes he lost. But no matter what, I would like to think that we were happy, even if it was only for a little while.

Soon after, the question of a visa was raised when the United States Customs officials kindly informed Oliver that the next time he left the country they would not allow him back in unless he had the proper paperwork. Now, all of our plans for the future were rushed. I wanted Oliver to stay. He did not want to leave. And so, on the ride home from the airport we planned our wedding.

On the 29 of April 2007, we were married in my backyard underneath an arbor built by my father. Here in the place where memories are made and the place where memories are kept, only the intimate were gathered. Reveling in the opportunity to relive moments from childhood, we put on the Muppets because today was the day that that somebody that was getting married was me.

As I got ready I felt like a little girl doing all of the things that only adults are supposed to do. I put on my wedding gown, a cotton dress with spaghetti straps and an empire waist; a dress I knew that I would ruin and it was not long before a whole glass of cabernet sauvignon was spilled down the front, turning this white dress into crimson. Around my neck I wore my mother's pearls and my left ring finger awaited the ring that Oliver had bought just the week before. Shosholoza played as I walked barefoot down the aisle. Somewhere over the voices of Ladysmith Black Mambazo, my father, ever the philosopher, tried to impart words of wisdom on this most sacred of days, but the aisle was too short and his words were left unsaid. Was he trying to teach me all that I had yet to learn about love? That there is a difference between a beautiful wedding and a beautiful marriage and that one can most certainly be had without the other.

Oliver's best friend Kyle flew in only the night before just in time to deliver the best of best man speeches where he offered a lobola of a single cow, which in actuality was a stuffed animal, and a blessing in Xhosa. After, we danced to Ben Harper and we cut the cake, a three-tiered icebox cake ringed with purple orchids made from the magic that occurs when chocolate wafers and freshly whipped cream are placed side by side and left to their own delicious devices. It tasted the way my childhood tasted: sweet and soft, rich and dense, and impermanent, always impermanent.

Forever a believer in signs and symbols, yet another sign led me to the back Far East; this time Thailand to study Thai Yoga Massage. At the time, I was (and still am) a fitness instructor overcome by a desire to gain a deeper understanding of the human body and the human heart and with the hope that this ancient knowledge might be used to heal others as well as myself.

But maybe that was just an excuse for the fernweh that had returned- even though it never actually leaves- for no amount of time or stamps on your passport strips you of this ache. Oliver, despite my most desperate implorations to come with me, stayed in New York for there were houses to be built, television to be watched, and golf to be played. So much for our promises of travelling the world together.

Just after the New Year, I flew alone into Bangkok in the middle of the night. Even though the hour was late, all of Thailand was still awake. Along the crowded streets there were pushcarts peddling hot food and cold drinks and there were tuk tuks carrying passengers to and from their midnight revelries. The night was alive and yet, in the night there was darkness. Lady boys, ladies of the night, and young children, some no older than ten years old, stood on corners, waiting, watching, and hoping to profit from the all too wicked ways of the world. I wanted to avert my eyes and pretend that these were things that my heart willingly accepts as one of the darker truths in a misbegotten world, but I could not and so with difficulty I walked along Sukhumvit Road. That night, sleep did not come easy.

When morning arrived after too few hours of sleep another flight was taken from Bangkok to the northwest of Thailand: the city of Chiang Mai where massage school was to begin on Monday.

Before eight, students from all corners of the world arrived at the doorstep of our future school intent on learning this ancient tradition. Our morning ritual began with the washing of feet in a large basin followed by a prayer, which ended in: *Shanti. Shanti. Shanti.* Peace. Peace. Peace. Perhaps it was here that peace would finally be found.

In the afternoons, when school was finished, I walked down the dirt streets on the outskirts of Chiang Mai as the scent of lemongrass, kaffir limes, and coconut lingered in the air. In eventide, when the sky darkened from cobalt to gray, we took tuk tuks to have dinner in the city center. Once a restaurant had been found, we shared meals of spicy green curry laden with potatoes and cashews or Pad Thai served with crushed peanuts, limes and bamboo shoots. After, we wandered through the temples that were scattered throughout the city where statues of Buddhas, some reclined, others sitting in lotus position, waited for us to offer them our prayers as incense burned, symbols rang, and monks shuffled their feet here and there. When we grew tired, we returned to our hotels, to prepare for another day.

How I wanted Oliver to be here so that we could go on an adventure- one of the many that we were supposed to have in our life together- so that when we returned to New York, winter would not be so cold and the wind would not be so bitter. But he did not come. He was there and I was here and we were so very far apart.

With days to fill before my return flight to New York there was one last place that needed to be visited, for it is difficult not to visit a wonder of the world when you are so very close. Under the cover of night I flew to Cambodia with no place to lay my head once arrived. A motorbike was hired upon leaving the airport and we drove toward the center of town, which was no more than scattered buildings built upon dirt roads. In the tropical night, clay and dirt rose from the tires as we passed palm trees and families of four on one motorcycle going in the opposite direction. A hotel was found for the equivalent of about ten American dollars for a night. Outside small fires burned in oil drums and voices were carried off into the Cambodian darkness. Inside the light above the single bed buzzed, competing with the fan that rattled, shook, but did not turn, leaving the stagnant air as it stood. The tiled floor of the bathroom was slightly pitched, allowing the water to flow into the toilet, which also served as a drain. Not soon after a brisk shower, I crawled into the twin bed and slept a sound sleep.

Just after the sun rose I rented a bicycle and rode for miles to the ruins of Angkor Wat; a city built in the twelfth century to venerate Lord Vishnu, protector and preserver of the universe. There, courtyards are overrun by banyan trees and their exposed roots climb over and under the weathered sandstone sculptures as monks, dressed in their saffron robes, meditate in stillness and silence.

Moving further and further away from the earthly representation of Mount Meru, I climbed the steep and narrow steps of smaller temples to look out across what once was as the tropical sun beat down upon the hard stone and earth. Perspiration had gathered across my brow and sweat ran down my spine by the time I reached the top where below, elephants roamed; their bodies aged and caked with dust and mud, looked almost as ancient as the faces of gods carved into the stones who watched over this place.

And still, among the ruins, was war made visible. There were men without his arms or legs begging for food, children without parents selling flowers and souvenirs, and signs warning of the dangers of walking through unswept mine fields. These were the remnants of the Vietnam War and reminders of the cruel regime of Pol Pot, under whom one-quarter of the population of Cambodia was expunged over the course of the four years of the Cambodian Genocide. But the genocide did not end in 1979, for the landmines that were left behind still claim the lives and limbs of Cambodians all these years later.

Whatever it was that I knew about Cambodian history was learned from reading *First They Killed My Father: A Daughter of Cambodia Remembers* by Lung Ung, the story of a young girl that survived the Khmer Rouge and *Emergency Sex and Other Desperate Measures* by Kenneth Cain, Heidi Postlewait, and Doctor Andrew Thomson. What more there was to learn about the Cambodian Genocide took place in Phnom Penh.

There, I stayed at a hostel adjacent from Tuol Slung: the notorious prison that the Khmer Rouge used for their most horrific methods of torture. In silence I stood in these classrooms turned torture cells that were furnished with only a single bed of box springs and no mattresses. Blood stains the floors, serving as eerie reminder to all who visit of the crimes committed here. Photographs of the unforgotten hang in the common area of Security Prison 21, their faces revealing the cruelties they endured in this place and their eyes imploring all of those who return their gaze to never forget.

Once made aware that places such as this exist, it is enough to make you sick with grief, it is enough to make you weep, it is enough to make you rage against a past which has continued far too long into the present, not only in Cambodia but elsewhere. Everywhere.

When I returned to New York, my body knew not the difference between day and night so in the early hours of the morning, when sleep kept its distance, I watched *The Killing Fields* and as the story unfolded on film and light began to ascend upon this side of the world, I stayed awake with thoughts of what war, violence, and fear do to the hearts of men. But perhaps it was not the difference in time that roused me from my restless slumber, but the thought of how little can be done to stop the madness of men. The movie ended. The sun rose. And still: *Nessun dorma.* No one sleeps.

For what remained of that winter I, too, became consumed with madness, a madness in which Oliver became my sole target. Our arguments, of which there were many, did not always determine who was right and who was wrong. More often than not they were only contests in which we competed with one another to see which one of us was more stubborn. Little did we know that no one wins silly contests such as these. At twenty-six I was still angry with the world, and this anger manifested itself into screaming and yelling and the slamming of doors and behaving like a child in the hope that he would see through all of my lunacy and into the very depths of my the pain. But he, too, was blinded by his own pain, which was so very different than my own and neither of us was ever able to soothe the other.

That May we went to London to visit his family and celebrate his thirty-first birthday and it was there that I began to use a new word among my ever-growing lexicon of useful marriage phrases; a word that stems from the Latin *divortium,* to separate and from the French *divertere,* to leave one's husband.

From Oliver, I wanted a divorce.

And then he left. I was the one who told him to leave. I was the one who told him he could not stay. It was a September that he arrived and it was a September that he departed. There were a thousand days in between. I did not take him to the airport. He would not let me, perhaps because I would no longer let him call me his wife, or, perhaps because all of our memories began at airports and this memory, this memory would be our last.

Divorce is just the most awful way of saying goodbye.

In October, as leaves died in the arms of tress and the nights grew long and cold, I lay awake in the middle of our bed, now my bed, struggling between having made the right decision and having made a mistake. When the hour was more appropriate, I called him. He was in London. These are the things that I said:

I miss you.

I made a mistake.

These are the words that were said after I hung up the phone:

I still love you.

I will always love you.

I will never stop loving you.

And these are the words that I never spoke out loud:

I am sorry that I do not know enough about the human experience and the human
heart to understand and maybe even accept who you are and who I am.
I am sorry that I loved you opaquely and not translucently.
I am sorry that my heart knew not the difference.

At that time I did not know any of these things for youth is only given
a finite amount of gifts and a seemingly infinite amount of time.

Wisdom is never bestowed upon the young.

On Divorce

Soon after, the leaves fell and then the snows and it was winter. It was a winter without the sun, without warmth, without Oliver.

The envelope was postmarked December 24.

I knew what it was and still, I opened it.

Papers with his signature.

Papers with my signature.

Some inks are permanent.

That Christmas, for the first time, there were only five of us eating leftovers at an otherwise empty table.

My winter had begun.

January arrived and with it a new decade. Overcome by an indescribable grief, there were the days where I found myself on the floor, unable to escape from the ground that constantly gave way beneath my feet where I learned that sometimes the bottom is not always made of rocks, sometimes there is no bottom at all.

Determined to find answers where often there are none, I continuously researched the Kubler-Ross model in order to construct a timeline of just how long it would take for me to get over Oliver, as if divorce was a chronological event in which progress is made from one stage to the next without relapsing into previous stages. Denial. Anger. Bargaining. Depression. These first four I had down to an art form, especially anger, but the last one, acceptance that was going to take a while. I did not know it then just how overrated anger actually is.

In those nights too long and those days too short I did not know the difference between struggle and surrender and so at all hours of the day I showed up on my mother's doorstep and crawled inside of her arms begging her to take my pain away, to make it stop, but she could not do any of that. All she could do was hold me and tell me that not all love was lost. Just one. Just one.

Then, as now, as always, my mother was and is my sun, my moon, my north star, my Southern Cross, my light in the darkness except she is the opposite of gravity. When I fall, when any of us have fallen, she pulls us up.

That winter I went to Paris, even though this was not something that I could actually afford, especially since I had my bank on speed dial just to determine whether or not food was a viable option on the days in between my paychecks. But still, I went to Paris nevertheless with my old friend Nina to stand in front of the Eiffel Tower again just as I did before all of this began without knowing how it would end.

Of course, like a fool, I went to London first, because it was cheaper and easier to fly to England- never mind the fact that enough miles had been earned over the years for a free flight to anywhere in Europe- and because that is also where Nina lived. It was most certainly not because Oliver was there and I still loved him, definitely not because of that.

In January, I found myself in his flat sitting across from my now ex-husband as he held a new book in his hand. He wore reading glasses and around his wrist there was new tattoo, so different than the tattoos that stretched between his shoulder blades and graced the cuneate muscles of his arm. That night, I slept on the pullout couch in the living room as he slept in his bed upstairs. In the morning he woke me up before he left for work to say one final goodbye. He kissed me on the cheek, close to my lips, with his hand lingering on my hip. He smiled as he walked out the door, never to be seen again.

After Paris, I returned to an apartment empty except for the memories that hung in the air and a lifetime of books on the shelf. All too willing to remain in the darkness of my own making, I lit few candles and stared at the titles that leaned against the wall. In the flickering light the wings of a butterfly caught my eye. *Papillon*. This was the book that Oliver was reading the night that we first met and, as I leafed through its pages, I wondered whether it was the imprisonment that Oliver identified with the most or was it the escape?

Unable to understand or accept the ambiguity of this life, I went outside and pulled a cigarette from the pack that I bought for moments such as this and lit one cigarette and then another and watched the rings of blue smoke rise into the cold, cold night.

Not easily overcome with religious zeal or political fervor, but terrified by my own heartache and spellbound by the ends of the cigarettes

217

burning harsh and red, I decided to have a *falò delle cuoro;* a bonfire of my heart. Somehow I led myself to believe that if there was nothing left to remind me of Oliver that the pain would go away. That if I didn't have the letters that he wrote or the cards that he sent that I, too, could pretend that he did not exist.

So a match was lit and into the pyre went photographs of the two of us: Us dancing to Ben Harper on our wedding day, us returning to San Francicso after an afternoon of drinking cabernets sauvignons in Napa Valley, and us on the bow of a sailboat watching the sky go from blue to indigo to black to night. Us smiling. Us laughing. Us happy. Birthday cards. Love notes, not-so-love notes, and letters that told of a forever that ceased to exist. And as the last of the flames turned ashes into dust I thought to myself:

How tightly we cling to our failures. How lightly we embrace our successes.

Long after the fire went out, I held onto Oliver.

It took years to let him go.

On the Best of Summers

Somehow, life carried on. The winter, eventually she relented, and spring subtly took her place among the seasons as I took my place among the world that refused to stop because he was gone and my heart was broken.

Since I could not go back, the past is unforgiving in that way, there was no other place to go but the beach, that ancient refuge of paradise lost and paradise found, where one must always go to close those old wounds left open by the all too slow passage of time.

On the days without rain I found myself wading into the still cool water wishing for summer and searching for a sign among the waves that foretold of a future full of hearts unbroken. I do not know what it was that I was looking for out there in the harbor that could not be found on dry land. Maybe it was an instinctual mistrust of solid ground or a primordial need for all things fluid. Nevertheless, it was there that an answer was found in the most unexpected of forms. Life is funny that way, presenting us with gifts that we never asked for and never knew that we wanted or needed until they are received.

There it floated in the middle of the harbor. Like the clouds and the sky it was blue and it was white. It was a tiny island, a floating dock, in a sea of sorrow, inviting me to step beyond the safety of solid things. Of course I was curious to know from where it came or who put it there, but when days passed and no one laid claim to its edges my grief for what was overcame my guilt for what is and out I swam to trespass on what was not mine.

When I climbed onto the dock, soaking wet and slightly fearful of the distance between it and the shore, no alarms rang out, no sirens wailed, not a word was said. All was silent except for the water that lapped softly against the fiberglass and wood and I knew then that this was to become the place of my reckoning.

One perfect Saturday afternoon, fathers with their sons and daughters moored their boat close to the shore awaiting everyone to climb on board and it drifted closer and closer to where I lay trespassing. As they waited, the kids jumped in and out of the water, splashing, kicking, and crying out to one another, Marco! Polo! as I once did a lifetime before. Over the idling of the engine the men apologized for the ruckus their children were making and then said the most beautiful words that had ever been said that summer or any summer since:

"Hey, sorry that our kids are splashing around so much. Can we get you a beer?"
To which the only possible response on this most perfect of Saturday afternoons was "Fuck yes."[6]
"We have Heineken or Bud heavy. Which one do you want?"

I had to pinch myself for surely this was a dream. Not only was a beer being offered, but also being offered was a choice in the matter, a choice where,

---

[6] Let's be honest, the real response was "Yes. Please. Thank you." After all, there were children around.

although you are asked to forgo your beer snobbery, you are still able to choose a king among giants. So without hesitation I said: "I'll take the Budweiser." And with those oh so magic words he reached into the cooler for the King of Beers, which he tossed across the water into my all too willing hands. I thanked them for their kindness as their boat sped away leaving small waves in its wake, tiny ripples that still rock my soul to sleep to this day.

I twisted off the top, peeling what remained of the label from the glass. Where after, I raised the bottle to the sky, watching as the light of the sun refracted through the amber liquid, and in a *Mir zur feier*, I cheersed to this moment, I cheersed to the summer that would one day end, and I cheersed to the Great Mystery that surrounded me. And then, bringing the bottle to my sun kissed lips I took the longest of sips. It was cold and it tasted of salt and the sea and happiness and freedom. Somehow I wanted this moment to stand still in order to revel in this freedom forever, but that is not possible; time does not stop, time cannot stop. It is only our memories that persist and this memory is a forever memory.

After, I returned to this dock almost everyday. It was there, above a sea that was sometimes calm, sometimes chaotic, that that old dog Sirius, the brightest of summer stars, guided me through my darkness, as the tides rose and fell, rose and fell.

There was an afternoon, just before the sun set when the tide was high and the moon was full in the still blue sky when it was not yet dark, not yet night, that made it feel as if I was floating along the Grand Canal of Venice not as it is, but as it was imagined by Claude Monet. The sky above blushed its lilac and its apricot, embarrassed as it was that the hours passed too quickly and the day soon would fade. How still everything became in this moment, suspended as it was with no past and no future, there was only here and only now. It was then that I had remembered that there had been another great love before Oliver. There had been Art. And there had been other men whom I had loved before Oliver as well. Men named Tiziano and Rembrandt, Jean-Leon and Alessandro. These were the men who reminded me that there are indeed some loves that last forever and these loves can be always be returned to, always and perhaps these men, among countless others, could be studied once more.

So that summer before my thirtieth birthday, when an entire decade was soon to pass, the question was no longer why did things happen as they did? It thus became: How was life to unfold from this moment on? Was I willing to leave this sacellum in order to apply to graduate school and run the risk of being rejected? Of failing? Of falling short? Try as I might, I could not stay. This moment, this dock, this sorrow, this season was not to last.

By August, my heart no longer ached as it once did. For this dock that swayed back and forth, allowed me believe in magic, in mystery, and in wonder once again because it was this dock, even in my greatest moments of doubt and in my deepest moments of despair, when I thought I would drown, that kept me afloat. Often I thought of leaving a note, a message in a bottle, to whomever that dock belonged, but I never did, afraid that it might break the spell that had been cast. So instead, I said thank you to the winds, the waves, and the water.

And then, like August, it was gone.

When not on the dock the rest of the summer was spent dancing naked in the rain and sleeping without clothes out of doors, waiting for Venus to rise above the horizon, as stars and satellites appeared on by one in the sky. And when sleep eluded me, I returned to the beach and stripped down to all but my soul and swam beneath an ever-changing moon.

On the first of September, after an *Aestas Mirabilis*, I moved back into the home of my parents, those generous and gracious creatures, so that I could apply to graduate school. Having been out of school for almost a decade it was hard to tell whether or not the right choice was being made, but to stay and deny the dream dancing in my heart would have been the worst decision of all.

While I waited, I worked and while I worked, I waited. When spring began to show her impatience with winter and crocuses crept through the thawing earth, one rejection letter followed another until there was only one school that remained. When the letter arrived from the Savannah College of Art and Design I did not want to open it, fearful that it was yet another rejection, but it was a letter full of congratulatory remarks at being accepted into the Master's of Arts program in Art History: When would I like to begin?

In the waiting I went on a date here and a date there, most of which were one-date wonders, if they could be considered wonderful at all, but most nights were spent alone or in the company of friends and family. It must be said that one of the best pieces of advice that was ever received from my mother was to take my time and not get involved with anyone too quickly after my divorce for the heart needs time to mourn and grieve its losses before inviting in new loves. Besides, the best way to get over someone is definitely NOT by getting under someone else.

But that spring did as spring does. Stirs our souls and our loins and I began to crave that sweet spring nectar. Almost two years had passed and I thought that was more than enough time to grieve and heal and release the anger that remained. By then I thought that I had forgiven myself for losing, for failing, for quitting, for giving up. Loneliness leads us to believe all types of lies that we tell ourselves.

Working at a gym, I tried my darnedest to live by the soft rule of no shitting where I ate, but that rule went out the window on the day that he first walked past me on the stairwell with headphones in his ears. He wore a charcoal t-shirt, which wrapped tightly around his shoulders, revealing the undulations of his muscles, the curves of his back, the outline of his clavicle, and the protrusion of his laryngeal prominence. His hair was more black than brown, as were his eyes, and both were a shade darker than his skin, the color of caramel. My loins actually stirred as he passed and electricity coursed through my body. As he climbed the stairs I whispered, "*I love you,*" part of me hoping that he heard me, part of me hoping that he had not. When we finally spoke I pretended that this was only a single conversation and that it meant nothing more than two people making small talk after their workouts all the while attempting to ignore what big ears he had, what big eyes he had, and let us not forget those all too perfect teeth. And still, I gave him my telephone number, which he waited all but a half and hour to put to good use.

In March, we went on one date and then another. He came in like a lion and me, as always, went out like a lamb. When we kissed our lips and tongues spiraled into one another like a collision of universes, which disrupted all of my perceptions held of both time and space.

It was soon, too soon, that he started calling me his girlfriend. It had only been a few weeks since he had broken up with his last girlfriend of years and years. I thought perhaps that he might need time to let her go, but he insisted that he did not. So, despite not having a say in the matter, I was his new girlfriend and that was that.

He lived in an apartment that overlooked the harbor, which welcomed the first light of day and the first stars of night. From his window I watched as the sun rose over the island, at first rust and crimson, then brightening into flames of pink and gold. In his kitchen, coffee percolated in an espresso maker that had been bought when he lived in Italy some years before. When the whole of the island was bathed in light, I sat at his table drinking it all in, sip by searing sip, as my mind, not always the most rational of organs, attempted to have a conversation with my body who cares only of pulsations and sensations and little for logic, about what exactly it was that was happening here.

My intuition hinted that something was not quite right.
One cheek pleaded to the other: *"Don't turn. Don't turn. Don't turn."*
The left side of my brain did the math and most things did not add up.
My legs warned, *"Do not shave us for this man."*
My feet begged me to run away.
And my heart quietly whispered, *"He will only break us."*

And yet, that spring into summer I told all of them: my head, my heart, my feet, and my legs, to go fuck themselves. This mistake was mine to make. And what a mistake it was, at least for those first intoxicating weeks until his ex-girlfriend showed up at his apartment, drunk after midnight. That was when the first red flag was raised, but by then my white flag had already been offered. I had already surrendered. Thereafter, despite the best and loudest protestations that my head and my heart could muster, we spent almost everyday with one another, for it was our souls that longed to dance with one another.

So in this clash of souls we did as lovers do: We laughed. We drank. We cooked. We fed each other oh so many good bites. We kissed. We fucked, undulating underneath the weight of one another: limb-to-limb and skin-to-skin. Sometimes after, sometimes before, sometimes during, we watched *Spartacus* naked under blankets. We were never dressed.

In the lateness of the afternoons we swam across the harbor, the tide high, the water cool, and climbed onto the sunbaked jetty, letting beads of sea and salt pass between our lips. In the shallow water we played like children, skipping balls and rocks across the surface, making up games as we went. We stood bare of skin in front of the mirror as salt water dripped from our shoulders and down our backs, wondering just what it would be like when we were eighty-five, long after youth had broken all of her promises and years and time left their marks on our bodies and our hearts.

When the sun finally surrendered its light, we lit fires and watched the moonrise full and bright across the water, its reflection silver and blue upon the night blackened sea and fell asleep across from one another as soft breezes carried away these days of delight.

When it rained and passion found new forms of expression, I read to him from one of the (few) books on his shelf, curling up in his arms and telling him of the Tarahumara who ran barefoot through the hills of Mexico. If this was intimacy, this was enough for me, more than enough for me. How desperately I wanted to believe that this, too, was enough for him.

228

But not for him. Never for him. And yet, despite this incessant and instinctual siren that wailed and hissed and never subsided, I went back to him over and over again, as if degradation and humiliation were things to be sought after in a relationship and not things to be condemned.

On May 1st word reached the United States that Osama bin Laden had been killed. The manhunt was over. Since he was a patriotic man, this was a victory for him, for us, for the United States, and perhaps even the world. So as to "celebrate" we went to his favorite restaurant, sat at the end of the bar, and ordered two beers for the occasion. Waves of guilt washed over me as we toasted to the murder of this man who was responsible for the murders of so many, knowing all too well that his death would never bring back the dead and his death would never bring the peace we all seek. Violence only begets violence. When the hour grew late and the night returned with its darkness, we departed leaving what remained of our beers unfinished and drove home, not a word spoken between us.

In the days after the Fourth of July, he had somewhere else to be; it did not matter where. He was to be gone for a month. I 'volunteered' to stay at his apartment so that I could have a quiet place to write and he would have someone to take care of his dog while he was gone. The moment he returned we broke up, or rather he dumped me. I cannot say that I was surprised. Hurt, but not shocked. For the length of our relationship I entertained his excuses. I believed the lies that so easily escaped from his lips. I was even the one who rang the alarm when I saw that his pants were on fire. Just hours after he returned – had he ever really left? - I had been replaced, forgotten, and without my knowledge or consent, I had ceased to exist.

And yet for reasons I still, cannot comprehend, even to this day, I continued to go back for more. The first and last time he laid his hands on me I had convinced myself that it was I who was at fault for getting angry with him in the first place. Why could I not just have looked the other way? Maybe, if I had not reacted the way that I did, maybe had I not confronted him for his indiscretions, then maybe I would not now be finding myself on the floor, struggling to get up, get out, get away from him, but in those moments when strength and sanity depart, I was incapacitated by the fear that remained. How uneasily these patterns of abuse are broken.

From that day on, my father, forever finding a way to demonstrate how often history repeats itself, diabolically referred to him as Rasputin. A good psychotherapist might classify him as the Dark Triad; that perfect trifecta of narcissism, Machiavellianism, and psychopathy, of which there is no known cure. But since no psychology major was I and since this all took place in July of 2011, he was my He-Who-Must-Not-Be-Named, my Voldemort, and he used my heart as his horcrux.

It was not until long after this love affair came to a disastrous and dramatic, yet inevitable, end that I finally understood the difference between passion and possession. This wanton desire to be loved was desperate enough to drown myself in the belief that, *"That will never happen to me..."* Words that ring true until, until it happens to you.

It was in those months that I learned just how it is that women come to blame themselves for the flaws and foibles of others. Natural nurturers we have forgotten what instinct has taught us over the course of millennia:

230

That the most dangerous and vicious of predators are often the most beautiful as well.

After I moved to Georgia we never spoke again.

On Georgia

Three days after Christmas, I left for Georgia.

One of the last of the original thirteen colonies and among the first to secede from the Union, Georgia was the second Confederate state that I was to call my home for the sake of learning so much more than could be learned within the walls of academia.

After 858 miles, we arrived in this slumbering city long after dark to an apartment that looked like it had not been cleaned since Jefferson Davis last held office. But hey, this is what five-hundred and ninety-five dollars a month in rent gets you: a one bedroom apartment that ran parallel to one of the most travelled streets in Savannah with closets that had been converted into kitchens and bathrooms, a fireplace in which no longer held fires, and windows that had been nailed shut; whether that was to prevent those on the outside from getting in or those on the inside from getting out was yet to be decided. But it was only a block away from my academic building and just outside the bounds of the historic district, so maybe it was not so bad after all, except perhaps for the gunshots that went pop in the night.

On New Year's Day my parents returned to New York. Left now to my own devices, I imagined that it was only a matter of moments before my neighbors would welcome me with peach and pecan pies and that they would invite me onto their porches to drink sweet tea and mint juleps and talk about the weather and all sorts of southern pleasantries, but hospitality such as this was not to be experienced; not then, not ever.

School began with Contemporary Art. Aside from my fantastic professor, Doctor Holly Goldstein, I was the only other art historian in a room full painters and photographers, sculptors and architects, who were all contemporary artists. [7] Within the first hour of class the decade that had past since I last studied the history of art crash all around me and I began to doubt my decision to return to school. After all that time, how the heck was I supposed to know the difference between pre-modernity, modernity, modernism, postmodernism, post postmodernism, structuralism, and post structuralism? And didn't anybody call it the Renaissance anymore?

After over two hours my head began to spin and my brain began to ache; a malady that can only remedied by the lacing up of sneakers and setting out for a long run to explore the streets of this new city. On this January evening the temperature held above freezing even as the sun began its descent in the southern sky. In the twilight, grey clouds gathered above the oak trees as Spanish moss swayed in the wind. I ran down the sidewalk, finding my legs again after years of exercising only in gyms; how good these roads felt underneath my feet. Somewhere between 37th Street and Forsyth Park a man as dark as the approaching night was walking in my direction and it saddened me to think that fifty years ago this man would have been

---

[7] Professor Goldstein is included among the ranks of other fantastic professors: Dr. Rihab Bagnole, Dr. Arthur DiFuria, Dr. Geoffrey Taylor, Dr. Stephen Wagner, and my thesis advisor, Dr. Fredrick Gross. Thank you all for your passion and your patience.

expected to step off the sidewalk to allow me to pass because of the brutal laws of old Jim Crow and then I remembered that fifty years ago there would have been no need for him to do such a terrible thing because, then, if I were a thirty-two year old woman, the street was not where I would have been found, I would have been in the kitchen of my home preparing dinner for my family because that was what was socially acceptable of a woman of my age at that time.

In passing, we nodded to one another, perhaps both of us remembering that had it not been for those who fought their fights for freedom, that sidewalk might have remained empty, with neither of us being able to go in the direction of our own choosing. Still at the beginning of my run, I was made all too aware that despite how far we had come, we still had so much further to go.

In that magnolia spring it was easy to fall in love with Savannah: the way light penetrated the Spanish moss that hung from the boughs of the mighty oaks, the way the azaleas bloomed their pinks and purples, reds and whites, the way the wisteria climbed up the walls of houses made of brick and stucco, and who can forget those sweet, sweet scents of honeysuckles, Cherokee roses, and columbines hanging so thick in the air that on all of my walks and runs I had to stop midstride, close my eyes, and breathe so deeply of their perfumes in order to ensure that these moments became redolent memories that would stay with me always no matter how far the distance from their blossoms and now, even after the passing of years, I still long for those first sweet spring songs of cicadas and katydids, humming their hymns of the warmth to come.

237

When the day ebbed, Savannah brimmed with haunting light and haunting darkness. With Rachel, my huckleberry friend from graduate school, we walked the width and length of the city, through the streets, down to the river and back again, tracing the history of this old town past the place where Forrest Gump told all of us that life is like a box of chocolates, past an Olde Pink House, and underneath the boughs of sycamore trees that grew tall long before either of us had arrived in Savannah and would remain standing long after we left. Sometimes we stopped for samples of pralines at a candy shop along the way even though we had tried them hundreds of times before, always hoping that they were still warm and that the butter and sugar had not yet cooled on the marble slabs of the confectioner's counter.

And yet, despite the sweetness that was found in these moments, there was also an inexorable sadness in Savannah, which corresponded to my own sadness brought on by yet another self-imposed solitude. Sometimes, I like to refer to my time in Savannah as "*The Softening*", in which the edges of my being were smoothed and polished. Here, my anger eroded. My rage relented. In those first few months, when distractions were few, I finally began to talk slower, think slower, and live slower and slowly, Savannah was charming her way into my heart.

In March, Amanda, came to visit. After years apart we reconnected over shared memories and histories never forgotten. She came for St. Patrick's Day, a day in Savannah that compares with no other the rest of the year. An afternoon was spent at Tybee Island and after, we went to my new favorite bar where we met Tommy and where I met Hollywood.[8] Late in the afternoon we had our backs turned toward the crowd, entranced as we were in our game of photo hunt, but that did not matter for Tommy because he reached in between us and found what it was we had been looking for before our time had run out.

Tommy has blue eyes and blond hair and a gentleness that spoke of his Kentucky upbringing. Hollywood was quite the opposite. He stood at six feet with brown eyes and brown hair. He had the twang of Midwesterner and his easy smile only accentuated the one word that was written all over his face: TROUBLE. And not just any kind of trouble: my kind of trouble.

Together, Hollywood and Tommy were soldiers in the army and were stationed at Hunter Army Airfield. They had arrived in December, but here they were not to stay. In less than a week they were to deploy to Afghanistan to fight in a war that began when they were still teenagers and had yet to end. That night, Tommy and I promised to be best friends forever. Hollywood and I made no such promises. For us, in that moment, there was no war, there was only soft lips to be kissed, hard bodies to be pressed up against, and passionate love to be made, but only for this night. Just this once. And then he left.

For me, life continued as normal. Another quarter began and just ten weeks later it ended and school let out for the summer.

Born in the month of August, I am a child of summer and thunder and fireflies, but the summer of the South compares with no other. Here rises a heat that cannot be described without anger or bitterness for there is

---

[8] When it came to time to choose a name of his liking for this book, this is the actual name that he chose. That's Hollywood for you.

cruelty to the day when the winds refuse to blow and there is no refuge to be found in the shade. Even the stray cats, the lions of the south, crawling under the porches of houses, cannot escape the noonday sun. And yet at eventide, when the sky became golden and crowned the mighty oaks king for what remained of the day, the soft breeze returned from its diurnal hiding place bringing with it the night; a night that sang haunting melodies beckoning all who listen to come dance in its darkness.

For the rest of that summer, and all the seasons that followed, I rode my bike down up and down the Rails to Trails line; a small dirt path that ran alongside of the Savannah River towards Fort Pulaski before land gave way to sea. Along this six-mile stretch of land, marshlands and rivers, oyster beds and sandbars stretched out in all directions and it seemed as if Savannah went on forever. When I came upon the end of the line I stopped on the small wooden bridge that led nowhere to watch the ships come and go as dolphins flipped and jumped and played in the waters and ghost crabs scattered sideways across the sand and gravel before returning home again.

In this life I have discovered there are just some things that you cannot say no to:

The beach on a sunny day.
The beach on a not so sunny day.
The beach.
The beach.
The beach.
A good book when it rains.
A good book when it is not raining.

A cold beer.

Champagne for no reason.

And a twenty-five year old boy in a black pick up truck on a sultry Savannah night.

One night in March was all that it was supposed to be for that very same week he was deploying to fight in the war in Afghanistan and yet, when he returned three months later, August somehow became his month. He arrived at my apartment with a twelve pack of pumpkin beer under his bare and bronzed arms, which he carried with the ease of a soldier used to more difficult burdens. How ever could I tell him to leave?

Before the door was even closed to the world outside off came his shirt and then his pants and together we learned just how unnecessary clothes are in the fever of August. For what remained of the eighth month, we spent our days at the beach romping around in the surf and our nights allowing the heat of summer to pass between us. In the mornings we ate pancakes and drank coffee on top of the sweat soaked sheets as light cascaded across the floor of the apartment and on those sweet summer afternoons, succumbing to slumber and ceraunophilia, we lay naked in bed drifting in and out of sleep as thunderstorms came and went, came and went.

In September he was gone. He left for three months to train in the mountains of Georgia and the everglades of Florida. He left without saying goodbye. He came back in December, only to leave again less than four weeks later. Another deployment. Another departure without a goodbye. Perhaps it was easier this way for him, but not for me.

But then again, perhaps goodbye is all the more difficult to say when it is not known for certain if, when, or how one will return from war

241

or whether or not that war will ever leave you. But it is also difficult to stay behind knowing all the while that most wars are never worth fighting.

In the autumn, the reeds paled then turned gray and it was time to choose a thesis topic. This was supposed to be easy, scientific, and most of all, objective as my original intention was to study the intersections between art and physics, but I am neither easy nor objective nor scientific.

In the early weeks of the new quarter I came upon the photographs taken by photojournalists James Natchwey, Margaret Bourke White, Gilles Peress, and Alfredo Jaar. Some were black and white, others were color, and all spoke of the horrors and violence of the 19th, 20th and 21st centuries: the Civil War, Namibia, the Holocaust, Vietnam, Cambodia, Guatemala, Bosnia/Serbia, and Rwanda. These photographs spoke of the depths of human heartache. They spoke of pain and suffering, despair and sorrow, of losses without victories, and war without peace. Mostly, these photographs spoke to my insatiable need to understand war, both within and without, and a thesis topic was finally chosen: Art in the Aftermath of the Rwandan Genocide.

By that time, almost twenty years had passed since those horrific months of inhumanity and indifference. And again I wept. I wept because I knew that this time, at thirty-three, to witness no longer sufficed. Although excuses of ignorance and naiveté can so seldom be used in time of war, in April of 1994, I was only thirteen years old. And what is genocide to a teenager that knows next to nothing about the world in which she lives, let alone war? Then, whatever I thought I knew of Africa was learned from the *Lion King*. How easy it was as a child to believe that the whole of Africa lived by the motto of Hakuna Matata. But Rwanda is not the Pride Lands and life is not a Disney movie.

Over the course of the year writing about the genocide, there were desperate moments struggling to understand all that is wicked in this world. In a desperate attempt to shatter the truths that they held, books were thrown across the room. For months I read and reread accounts of unimaginable violence and incomprehensible loss, but there was also story after story of survival. These were stories of hope. This hope was what buoyed me up when I thought I would drown in the sorrows of genocide. And it was this was the hope that compelled me to journey to Rwanda after finishing my thesis because I needed to know that not all of life is war, not all of life is violence, and not all of life is loss upon insufferable loss, that there, too, is peace and beauty and resilience, and, above all, hope. And with that in mind, I planned a trip.

In this writing of a thesis a job was needed, so I took to waiting tables- something I had always done- at a restaurant on River Street in the heart of downtown Savannah. It was an old cotton warehouse whose very floors and rafters spoke of the unforgotten slave trade of the centuries before. There was a draft in the winter and a balcony without a breeze in the summer, which allowed the smell of stale beer to linger too long in the air. There were buckets in the middle of the table that held the broken fragments of oyster shells and the remnants of all-you-can-eat crab legs that were served as the Monday night special. These buckets, almost as old as the building itself, were coated in artificial butter and ranch dressing was forever sticking to the bottom, no matter how many times it was put through dish.

243

Obviously, no five star restaurant was this, but the opportunity to almost make my rent in one day was hard to pass up.

And besides, that was where I met Tex.[9] He stood in the kitchen behind the stainless steel counter expediting orders of shrimp po' boys, crawdads (otherwise known as mudbugs), and low country boils, all served on dented tin pans more resembling the tops of garbage cans than plates. He was a Southerner, not of the Southern Hemisphere, but a Georgia boy, through and through, who loved bulldogs and the Georgia Bulldogs. He had a ginger beard, blond hair, and a last name that ended in a consonant, but his eyes were every color blue and when he spoke he did little to suppress the softness of his consonants and the elongation of his vowels. He drove a Jeep Wrangler, which was a manual with the top down and the doors off, which had fun written all over it. On our first date we went to the beach and he made me a sandwich. Apparently, food and sunshine is all that it takes. I am that easy.

The next day I flew to New York for Lauren's wedding and it was beautiful and perfect, just like Lauren. When I came back to Savannah, Tex was in my kitchen with a bouquet of flowers, an open bottle of wine, and filet mignons dusted in salt and pepper, ready to be seared to rare perfection. Over dessert, I told him that I was leaving Georgia, that I never planned on staying in the South, that I was moving back to New York, and that I was traveling to Rwanda, all in less than a year. He did not put up a fight. He said only this: "That's ok. You are my summer girlfriend." It was only April.

Before the unforgiving southern sun baked the red clay earth dry, we went muddin' after a spring thunderstorm that soaked the roads and left puddles of shallow water in its wake. As we tore through backcountry roads,

---

[9] Tex is not his real name, but its pretty darn close.

the Jeep jostling and tumbling with every turn, I laughed and held tight to the 'oh shit' bar reveling in the simple pleasures of the south that I never knew until then.

In those early months of passion I had convinced myself that if I went for the opposite of what I usually go for then the opposite of what usually happens would happen. But wolves are wolves and sheep are sheep. Even after all of these years I have never been accused of thinking rationally, especially when it comes to matters of the heart (and the loins). But Tex was not without his merits. Puckish, he balanced the intensity of my thesis topic with his playfulness and his ultra laidback lifestyle, it was Tex who introduced me to the culinary delights of hush puppies: those golden nuggets of deep fried cornmeal without which any southern meal is incomplete, and it was Tex who taught me how to properly pronounce perhaps the greatest word in the English language, a word only Sammy Kershaw could sing about, and a word that can only be spoken with a Southern drawl. For this word is not only a word, it is a king among Plantae, an asparalagus of the highest order, a genius among all allium. Ladies and gentleman:

Vidalia.

An onion by any other name would definitely not smell as sweet.

For what remained of my time in Georgia, I stayed with Tex. But as I finished my thesis, the South, and Tex, began to lose their charm for in Savannah there is no such thing as silence. The humidity that lingers, even in winter, carries sound swiftly across the flat, unchanging landscape that stretches out in all directions, leading one to believe that maybe the world is not round after all. And at night, in this city of contrasts, it was almost

245

impossible to differentiate between the sound of gunshots and fireworks, in which one was often confused with the other, making it difficult to know whether one should proceed with caution or reckless abandon. There were also too many fervent believers in the second amendment and there were too many Confederate flags prominently displayed on the hoods of pickup trucks and hung on flagpoles in the front lawns of houses that spoke of a history unforgotten and apparently unfinished. There were also too many sentences that began with the phrase, "*I'm not a racist but...*" and ended quite the contrary. There were just too many words used all too casually for my Northern disposition.[10] Maybe, in the end, it was only the heat, unrelenting and cruel, that drove me from this inferno. Or maybe it was just that I missed New York. I missed my family with the same ferocity as how much I missed real pizza, driving at speeds faster than twenty miles per hour, and the changing of seasons from spring to summer to fall to winter and back again.

And so, just as the azaleas began to bloom, I left Savannah and everything that was there behind.

Had it not been for Magnolia trees in April, pralines, warm and sweet, in the afternoon, the way the light arched and bowed through the Spanish moss casting shadows over the streets of the city, the boom of thunderstorms that departed almost as quickly as they arrived, and winters without snow, maybe I would never have loved Savannah at all; for these are the things that I will take with me.

I may be a Yankee, but I will not be damned.

---

[10] This is not to say that racism only exists in the South. Even into the 21st century, and especially after the rise of dangerous movements, racism continues to exist throughout the United States and the world, and far from being eradicated it has found a new voice and a new presence among men.

On Rwanda

This final chapter is not about politics, nor is it a detailed account of the horrors of the genocide, of which there are too many to write about and there are only so many pieces that a human heart can break into before it is unable to be recognized as human at all. Therefore, this chapter does little to determine the difference between good and evil, for lines get blurred and are so easily crossed over and back over again until these lines are forever erased, leaving behind any notion of who was right and who was wrong.

Also, I am of the belief that no war is ever won. The losses that occur on both sides far exceed any victories. And thus far, almost a quarter of the way through the twenty-first century, we have learned nothing from violence and still have so much to learn from peace. So, for those who prefer their history to be told in the kind of chronological order destined for textbooks that are quick to declare a victor, I ask you to remember these words written by William Faulkner: "The field only reveals to man his own folly and despair, and victory is an illusion of philosophers and fools." But if it is a timeline that is preferred, I, and most historians will agree, will tell you that the genocide began on the night of April 6, 1994, when the plane carrying the Presidents of Burundi and Rwanda was shot down over Kigali.

Or did it begin in 1959? Or was it April 1972 or October 1993 in Burundi? Or did it continue for all of those years after in the Democratic Republic of the Congo? To keep it neat, I will say that the genocide took place for one hundred days claiming the lives of 800,000 Rwandans; such small, safe, even, round numbers. Besides, had the genocide continued longer, the amount of deaths would have far exceeded that of the Holocaust, for the Hutu rate of killing was three times that of Nazis.

But truth be told, the genocide did not end then, for wars do not end, they merely pause, and in their uncertainty of where to go next, they go everywhere leaving no land unmarred, no man unbroken, no woman untouched, no child unharmed. For war is cruel, war is reckless, war is ruination.

For too long after, both within the borders of Rwanda and outside of those lines of demarcation, war and rape and violence and rape and murder and rape and revenge and rape and greed and rape and disease and rape and displacement and rape and hatred and rape and rape and rape continued and the number of people who were killed during those one hundred days was multiplied by five-fold for the thousands of days to follow.

But I cannot speak to you about any of these things because of war I know nothing. I can only speak of my experiences twenty years later.

Just south of the equator beats the tiny heart of Africa. This heart is a country no bigger than the state of Maryland. Its earth holds no treasures of which to speak for there are no vast quantities of oil or minerals to extract from under its one thousand hills. The world does not depend any of its exports nor could much of the world point out its exact location on a cartographer's map. But still, this heart has a name and its name is Rwanda.

As of 2016, Rwanda is ranked among the poorest countries of the world with fifty-five percent of its population, roughly 6.6 million people living below the poverty line. With statistics such as these, there are some who argue that it is for these very reasons why no one, at least not immediately, intervened to prevent the genocide from occurring in 1994.

And it is also for these reasons that there were those that were 'Rwandering' why it was that I wanted to travel to a war torn country so very far away. For me, the answer was simple: Because it was what was in my heart and we must listen to our hearts so that we do not forget that we, too, have tiny hearts that beat inside of us.

Besides, for as long as I can remember, I have dreamt of Africa as often as I have dreamt of a world at peace. Since 1994, I arrived and returned from Rwanda countless times, but it was my heart that travelled across oceans and continents long before my feet found the earth of this land of one thousand hills; for it was my heart that ached and mourned for a country and a people who knew too much of violence, too much of war, and too much of hate for far too long.

On the first of May, my plane touched down in Kigali. Ten years had passed since last I set foot in Africa and my reasons for returning were so very different than a decade before.

Jet lagged, sleep deprived, and dehydrated after two days of travelling, I was not prepared to encounter so much beauty so soon, but Rwanda is a place where beauty is a thief: it steals the breath from your lungs and causes your heart to skip a beat. And it is here, among the hills of green beyond green and underneath skies of blue beyond blue, that it is difficult to tell where Rwanda ends and heaven begins.

After two hours of driving over the hills and through valleys on roads that were sometimes paved, sometimes strewn with rocks and dirt, I arrived in Gashangiro at the *Team Africa Rising* complex where, for the next two months, I was to teach English and yoga.

In the heat of sub-equatorial Africa I unloaded my bags from the trunk as corrugated tin roofs expanded and popped in the late afternoon sun and took stock of my new surroundings. At the edge of the compound a garden was in bloom, rich with cucumbers and spinach, rhubarb and summer squash. Eucalyptus trees, short and tall, thick and thin, cast shadows across the grass and gravel. The complex was bordered by a river to the west, a road to the east and to the north, volcanoes that separate Rwanda from Uganda and the Congo. How they rose from the hills obscuring all else from view. In this far away land everything seemed so near, yet so distant, all of it waiting to be discovered. But that would have to wait.

In Rwanda, the beginning of May marks the end of the wet season, but storms still gather in the mountains. There is no thunder; there is no lightening, only a shift of wind and then the rains. When they come the whole of Rwanda disappears underneath boughs of trees or eaves of barbershops. But these are only temporary shelters for these rains do not last and are soon replaced by the cool clear nights of the mountains of night. And so, in the coming and going of the rain, I soon fell asleep.

The next morning and every morning that followed I was awakened by the shrill cry of an Ibis piercing through what remained of the night, the low of cows let out to pasture, and the bleating of goats rising above the hushed voices of farmers already in their fields. So at first light I opened my eyes to this new world just as the sun crested its way over Mount Muhavura.

In town, I was to teach English at a sewing cooperative. The school was only four kilometers from the compound, so partly out of stubbornness and mostly out of curiosity, I walked the hour down the hill in the morning and the hour up the hill in the afternoon because it has always been my belief that when traveling the feet see just as well as the eyes.

I did not know what to expect of the world into which I stepped so I decided to expect nothing at all. Although I had been to countries where genocides had occurred, where humanity was all but forgotten: spending a day in Dachau, a week in Cambodia, Rwanda was different: more intimate, more recent, more immediate and although I placed one foot in front of the other I neither knew where I was going nor what it was exactly that I was doing. But this trepidation was what allowed me enter into this world that was not my own with an open mind and an open heart. And so I walked.

In Gashangiro, the main road is paved and lined with houses made of concrete and dirt, sometimes surrounded by shrubbery and fences, sometimes so close to the road that you can almost step off the pavement and onto the doorsteps. Dotted along this landscape are cabarets, decorated as they are with advertisements for cellular phone companies and local beers. Both in and out of doors there are shops and small tarps that sold tomatoes, sweet potatoes, and even shoes that were worn well past their welcome as charcoal burned and laundry hung to dry on bushes and trees.

Men, young and old, passed riding their single speed bicycles. Sometimes they were alone and sometimes they carried passengers. More often they pushed their bikes uphill, the tires flat and the frames bent from bearing the weight of hundreds of journeys such as this. There were also men who stood in large groups on the side of the road. Some casually held their pangas in their hands, others leaned on posts, but most shifted their weight from side to side growing boisterous in one moment and quiet the next, making it all the more difficult to tell what it was they are waiting for.

On either side of the road there were the mamas who swaddled their children on their backs as they worked in the fields, hoe in hand and perspiration gathering at their brow as their babies slept in their cloth cradles. More women, dressed in *mushanana,* made their way up the hill carrying freshly cut stacks of wood or bundles of cassava leaves upon their heads and yet, despite their burden, they did not fall, they did not falter, even as the sun penetrated the day and the rains fell without cease. Watching them on their journeys it was enough to make you wonder why it is that some are more able to bear their burdens than others.

Everywhere there were children. There were school children in green and white uniforms that followed me closely, intrigued as they were by the white woman walking down the street. The girls laughed, the sound of their slippers flipping and flopping against the pavement while the boys, more bold, spoke to me in near perfect English or broken French asking all kinds of questions that I tried my best to have answers for.

All along the way shrieks of *Muzungu! Muzungu!* were heard from the children not yet of age to attend school. Under the sun of a thousand hills they played soccer with balls constructed from plastic bags tied together with string, they pulled trucks made from cracked containers using broken caps as wheels, and they jumped in and out of gutters without shoes and sometimes without pants and almost always without parental supervision. The Westerner in me wanted to stay with them to make sure that they did not hurt themselves or fall too hard, but who was I to assume that despite their appearances of youth that they were unable to take care of themselves or that somehow I was better equipped to take care of them? Besides, these children never stopped smiling, and left with no other choice, I smiled back. And that month I discovered that these smiles, these fleeting moments of joy are often the most profound along this road, for they are formed from the same folds of life which also hold sorrow and sadness, and it is these smiles that make this daily journey all the more worthwhile.

But these smiles did not always linger long on my lips. In a place where running water is a privilege and electricity is not always guaranteed it was difficult not to see poverty everywhere in Rwanda. This poverty was made more than apparent in the clothes worn by men and women, young and old. There are clothes that have been passed down through more than one generation. Here, coats and jackets were worn that speak of seasons that do no exist in this climate. There were t-shirts that were previously worn by other people in other countries that live other lives. Looking out across this human landscape of Rwanda is like gazing upon an entire army in search of salvation.

Confronted by this poverty it seemed as if each moment contradicts the next and I could not help but get caught up in the space between

255

desperation and exaltation, contempt and contentment, frustration and redemption. In those days of walking, I feared that I had begun to suffer from the emotional bends due to this constant plunging and resurfacing of these contradictory emotions. But these sudden contradictions; I had to accept them all. Part of me, most of me, wanted to turn and look away from this poverty, to put on my sunglasses in order to hide my tears in fear that my weakness could never match their strength, but I could not because the people of Rwanda exhibit a resiliency bordering on the miraculous and it is a resiliency that I get to witness *bwimuzi, bwimuzi* (everyday, everyday).

It was also in those first few days of walking I tried to differentiate between those who were Hutu and those that were Tutsi. But you can only do this for so long before you begin to drive yourself mad with fear and sadness and grief. Somewhere along the road I stopped trying to guess who was a Tutsi and who was a Hutu because they are all Rwandan and they are all, in one way or another, survivors. And on these roads there is no going back. There is only going forward. And like me, these Rwandans are just trying to get up the hill because twenty years on, the people of Rwanda must continue to live together side by side, regardless of the past. In order to do so, they must forgive the unforgivable. Walking along these roads I question my own capacity to forgive and I fear that I hold on more often than I let go. I, too, have known anger and hate and rage. I am reluctant to forgive or even accept the things that I cannot control. Resentment still resides in my heart. But maybe here in Rwanda, this is the road to forgiveness.

When my whole being becomes overwhelmed and I grew to fear my next thought, I sought solace in the beauty that surrounded me. It was a beauty that was discovered in the hills that are in constant competition with the sky. It was found in the sky that shifts from steel to cobalt to indigo and back as the sun comes and goes from behind the clouds. It was a beauty that was found in the trees that remain forever green in this land of constant spring. But where beauty truly was triumphant was in the flowers. Whether they grow wild or are tame, the presence of their crimsons, their yellows, their pinks and their purples, especially their purples, brought a sense of serenity to these often-chaotic hills.

Walking up these hills, I was reminded of a conversation that I had with Chilean artist Alfredo Jaar before I departed. In August of 1994, Jaar had traveled to Rwanda in the wake of the genocide to document the violence and he spent the next six years coming to terms with all that he had witnessed. Unable to enter another church, another school, another home to document the violence he turned his camera to the clouds, the field, the road and I thought of him as I walked past these fields of flowers. Alice Walker also comes to mind: *"I think it pisses God off if you walk by the color purple in a field somewhere and don't notice it."* These fields, the color of purple, reminded me to notice everything, to notice it all because this is life, this is all of life and there cannot be light without shadows just as there cannot be shadows without light.

After an hour of walking down the hill, I arrived at the small compound off of the dirt and rock road that ran parallel to the main street of Musanze. Here I was greeted by a group of women who gathered together, Monday through Friday, to learn English and weave colorful baskets made of grass and twine. The day began with a warm embrace, repeated three times, cheek-to-cheek, before the offering of a half high-five/half handshake. So much of me wanted this greeting to be OUR secret handshake, but this was no secret; this is simply the way friends in Rwanda say hello.

All of these women were survivors of the genocide. In many instances, their parents had been killed, their children had been murdered, and their sisters and brothers were gone. Entire families were lost never to be returned and they were all who remained. I tried to imagine what that might be like, but that was impossible. And still, somehow, the lives of these women continued. At the co-op, they learned English, they smiled, they worked hard, and one day, they hoped to open up shops of their own.

Sometimes, on the way back, when I was brave enough, I climbed on the back of a motorbike, the helmet too big, the road too narrow, and my fear so great that I wanted to shut my eyes tight so as not to see the potholes we barely missed, the gutters we almost fell into, or the trucks coming straight towards us from the opposite direction. But to shut my eyes, I could not see all of the things that I was there to witness, even that which is difficult to see.

In the afternoons, I taught English and yoga to the group of young men who were all part of *Team Africa Rising*, the National Cycling team. These cyclists, the sons of both Hutus and Tutsis, came together to become part of a team and it was these young men from all over Rwanda, some who had never traveled further than the road to Musanze, who understood more of my language than I did of theirs.

Most days, the lessons went smoothly, but there was one day where frustrations ran high, for that was the day I learned just how audacious it was for me to come into their country and expect them to speak a language that was not their own. Who was I to perpetuate the belief that if they spoke English their life would improve? As if their fluency in Swahili, Luganda, and French was not enough. Was this just another byproduct of colonial rule? Or some sort of Neo Intellectual Colonialism in which, despite their

258

lack of sovereignty to a nation other than their own they were still subjected to linguistic rule? To make light of so heavy a quandary, I did as any teacher who had just been schooled by one of her students would have done; I turned to the universal language of music, this time choosing Wilson Pickett for the honors and, as the saxophone wailed and the snare drum rolled, they did the Watusi, just like little Lucy.

That day the land of one thousand hills became the land of one thousand dances.

That night, that clear, clear night, the power went out in Musanze and the Milky Way appeared, spreading itself out across the southwestern sky, blanketing the whole of Rwanda underneath a veil of stars. Here in East Africa, along its Eastern edge, I questioned why it is that physicists attempt to understand distant galaxies when it is so evident that we have yet to understand why things happen as they do on this small, obscure piece of real estate called Earth. Why it is that war, famine, and disease spread sometimes like tornadoes, sometimes like earthquakes, and sometimes like hurricanes, destroying almost everything in their paths and then, in these very same places, on nights when no rains fall, you can stand infinitesimally small underneath a canopy of heaven and experience the most profound moments of peace. Perhaps physicists and astronomers are simply human beings using a little bit of fire and a little bit of light to help us find our way in the dark.

After dinner some of the boys from the team lingered outside in a world temporarily removed from the pressures of cycling and school wondering just how it is that these stars do not all fall from the sky. In their innocence and in the darkness it is easy to forget that these boys, now men, were made witness to Rwanda's darkest hour and still their eyes are able to gaze upon the heavens and see all of the beauty and all of the wonder of the world.

The contrasts of this country are inescapable and I often get lost in the confusion of the night. In these moments I felt, as Isaac Newton must have felt when he revealed: *"I can predict the movement of heavenly bodies, but I cannot predict the madness of men."* But then I remember that night, too, has its certainties. For this planet is only a microcosm of the cosmos, expanding and contracting, exploding and imploding, shining brilliantly one moment only to fade into the next, all within the tumultuous rhythm of the universe.

Comforted by these thoughts, I make my way toward shelter and sleep. The hour is late and as I close my eyes I am lulled to slumber by the sounds of motorbike tires coasting down the hill with their engines off and the soft shuffle of feet finding their way home in the darkness as a the bark of a dog temporarily disrupts the nocturnal symphony that will continue until morning.

If we are to believe, as Rwandans do, that god sleeps in Rwanda, then these must be his lullabies. Tonight, dreams come easy.

In the waking hours of daylight, with only a single star to guide my way, I came to the realization that these contrasts are the ways in which the world presents itself to us: through struggle and survival, war and peace, pain and perseverance, joy and sorrow, toils and triumphs, mercy and grace. It may be that we live in a world full of contradictions, one that can sometimes seem unjust, imbalanced, nonsensical and absurd, but it is still the only world that we know. So bounded in this unbounded universe and left with left with no other choice, I choose only this: give me all or give me nothing.

In Rwanda, not all of my time was to be spent in the mountains for there was still a city to be explored and a thesis to be further researched. With one-week left of my journey I travelled to Kigali to seek perhaps the most hopeful of all: the artists of Rwanda. Here, the capital is alive with young painters and sculptors who believe in the Rwanda of their present and not the Rwanda of their past. And yet, to write of these experiences will be another book entirely.

My first destination upon arriving in Kigali was the Genocide Museum; a sun bleached building that stands on top of a hill, which is surrounded by gardens rife with equatorial flowers in constant bloom. In the midst of all this life there is a mass grave that holds the remains of at least 250,000 victims of the Genocide, their bodies interred so that the world may never forget the violence that occurred in this place.

On the walls inside hang photographs of schoolchildren and portraits of families, all snapshots of a time that came to a violent and bitter end. There is a room piled full of clothes, machetes, and other weapons of war used by the genocidaires. They are all stained with blood. In another room there are bones: tibias and femurs cleaved in half, fractured and shattered skulls, fragments of calcium and marrow, all morbid reminders of just how gruesome and unforgiving war can be.

Television screens upstairs spoke of the countless genocides that occurred throughout the twentieth century: Armenia, the Holocaust, Cambodia, and Bosnia-Serbia. Here, madness falls like rain and as I watched the deluge of history repeat itself time and time again the world over, I began to lose hope and I almost began to believe after being

261

confronted with so much anger, with so much rage, and with so much war that nothing can be done to stop such violence for we who want only peace are too few and THEY who wage only war are too many.

Fragile creatures, all of us, we are given hope and we are given fear in equal measure, and we can only hold on to one at a time.

But in this moment of despair I also remembered that, since the Genocide, Rwanda has embarked on a program of reconciliation; they have set forth on a journey of forgiveness. And this road is neither straight nor short nor simple. Where it leads no one is certain, but perhaps if we all walk together we might one day learn that it is WE who are the many and they are the few and Everything can be done to stop such violence.

After leaving the museum, I wandered through the streets where there were constant reminders of the genocide: the Parliament Building riddled with the bullet holes of AK-47's and RPGs, men without limbs, a sign outside of a church indicating that violence had occurred inside its sacred walls. No matter where I went, it seemed as if the past was inescapable until I walked into Inema Arts Center. On a hill overlooking Kigali I was greeted by the sound of blues and jazz, a confluence of rhythm that brought to life the canvases that splayed the kaleidoscopic colors of this country. Here are the burnt sienna's of the clay earth, the yellows of the African sun, blues like the shadows of twilight, and greens like the skins of unripened mangoes or the leaves of trees that know no other season but spring. And there are the reds and oranges like the fires of passion that burn ever so brightly in the hearts of these young artists. These were the colors of hopes and dreams. These were the colors of Rwanda.

It was there that I met two brothers: Innocent and Ema, both incredible artists, among countless other incredible artists, whose dream, now a reality, it is to return hope to Rwanda one stroke of paint at a time.

262

So full of light and love they were that it was easy to fall under their passionate spell and for hours we spoke about the necessity of art in the aftermath of tragedy and that creation must always follow destruction no matter how difficult of an endeavor that may be. All too aware that they cannot rewrite history, these brothers, as well as so many other Rwandan artists, are indeed writing the future of Rwanda. And I believe that it was Tony Cyizanye, artist and owner of Yego Art Center, who said it best:

"I paint in color so that the whole of Africa is not seen as darkness."

Upon hearing his words those fault lines of my soul began to tremor once again and that old familiar earthquake rippled through my bones. Here, in these studios, there is no darkness. There is only light.

As my time in Rwanda drew to a close there was one last adventure to be had for there were mountains that rose in the near distance calling to be climbed. So on my last Saturday in Rwanda, Daniel, another volunteer who coached the cyclists, and I decided to climb Mount Bisoke. Standing at 3500 meters, Mount Bisoke is the lesser of the Virungas, but still the place where gorillas play in the mist. Daniel is from Colorado and climbs mountains for fun. I live at the level of the sea. There are no mountains from where I come, only valleys and oceans. Everything before this was only a hill. Since this was to be the first mountain that I ever climbed, as we set out on our adventure we arrogantly asked our guide:

"What was the fastest that you ever made it to the top?"

"Two and a half hours," he answered proudly, knowing all too well that without us, he could do it in less. One look was all it took for both of us to know that this was a time that we could beat. Competitive athletes to the core we still sought after the edges of our limits. Little did I know that this is no way to approach a mountain.

And so we set off into the jungle surrounded by our guides in their khaki cargo pants and their waterproof boots over natural stairs created by protruding roots and a ground that was never dry. With each step my feet slowed and my heart beat faster. Bisoke took the breath from my lungs and the words from my mouth. Our guides, young men who grew up in these hills, thought nothing of this small mountain as their rifles hung casually at their sides and their strides neither shortening nor lengthening. Every now and again we stopped just long enough to take small sips of water and gaze upon the surrounding vistas of jungles and valleys. And then we continued upward, each step more dizzying than the last. Somewhere along the way, I lost faith in my own athletic ability. My legs are strong but short. My strides are small. My excuses are few yet many. And yet each step, met with hesitation and resistance, took us further and further up the mountain. The air grew thin and cold as I stumbled and faltered, grappling for roots and rocks, moist from the tropical rain, to keep me steady. Never fully rising above the tree line, we came to the place where the earth meets the sky and we found ourselves standing along the edge of a dormant volcano. Here, the fog never lifted, but crept silently across the mountaintop obscuring all else from view except for the Cape buffalo that hid among the vegetation that rimmed the crater's edge.

It is no small wonder that Rwanda lies along a convergent boundary; a place in which the contradictions and harmonies of this world come together to dance along this edge called life. Here, in this place of convergence, where fire and earth meet the sky, are whispered the old

264

universal truths of creation and destruction, agony and ecstasy, beauty and barbarity. And here in this cradle of civilization, where all of humanity is said to begin, we emerge and return from whence we came once again.

At the top of the world we stayed for only a few short moments before the warmth of our perspiration turned cool in the mist causing our teeth to chatter and goose bumps to rise to the surface of our skin. On the way down as I slid in mud so thick that my shoes and clothes became caked in dirt, I thought to myself how quickly we are able to descend, how slow our ascent. And so, it was not with pride that I came down from the mountain. It was with humility and one thing was for certain: this mountain, this country, these people, had made me humble and it brought to brilliant and devastating light all of the things that I am, all of the things that I am not, and everything else in between and for that I grow ever more grateful.

After, Daniel and I went down to Musanze to buy a beer in order to properly celebrate the mountain. When we walked into the small store that sold wet and dry goods, toiletries, and produce, there it stood in the cooler in between the Tusk and the Primus, a remnant of another lifetime in Africa: a Savannah Dry. And in this pentimento place where Savannah meant something else, something less recent, something more distant, I remembered:

I remembered that once, not so long ago, my feet had touched this land of mysteries and magic, a little further south, a little further west.
I remembered how we used to drink this cider as we watched the sun sink into the ocean, waiting, always waiting, for that spark, that green flash to electrify the sky, telling of another day gone by.
I remembered Oliver.

I remembered him.

And so I bought a cold bottle and offered a toast to what once was and will never be again and raised the glass to my lips. The cider had lost none of its sweetness. The taste it left was no longer bitter for Rwanda was no place for my anger. And for the first time in years, I smiled as I thought of him and when the once tangerine sun turned pink then flushed purple with the mountains I finally let him go.

Now, I know only this to be true:

Not all loves are meant to last, most are ephemeral and fleeting at best, but all that is asked from each of us is to love as much as you can for as long as you can...

For love, all love, is wild and cannot be tamed.

In Kinyarwanda there is a phrase that defines a journey: *buhoro, buhoro,* step-by-step. And it is these small steps, taken ever so slowly which eventually lead us to where we are supposed to be. What we find along the way may surprise us, it may confound us, it may disquiet us, but it also might arouse in us something that lay too long dormant, something that we never knew lay sleeping inside of us longing to be awoken. For there are mysteries at work in Rwanda, both forgotten and unforgotten, that remind us there are depths and there are heights that we have not yet reached; but, maybe, just maybe, one day, we will.

And so, as I continue these revolutions around the sun I have come to realize that no matter how near or how far I travelled it was never the destination that mattered. What I sought were the real wonders of the world: beauty and magic, mystery and miracles, faith and wisdom, love and laughter, and, above all else, hope. Always hope. And I have found all of this and more along the way. Now there are only two words that I repeat over and over and over again, day in and day out, until my very last breath:

Thank you. Thank you. Thank you. Thank you. Thank you. Thank you.

For it is only now, as I pull thirty, that I have learned that much of my life has been spent hiding behind a seemingly insurmountable wall of anger whose very depths were matched only by its height, heights which cast unwaning and unwelcome shadows across the landscape of my heart. Perhaps all along, I had been searching for the gates of grief through which we all must walk to the place beyond the wall where there is light, where there is hope, and where there is love.

Neither plane nor train can take us there. There are no station stops or road signs to guide our way. We must set off as we set off on all of our journeys, with one foot in front of the other, in the direction of the sun.

I am taking the long way home.

ACKNOWLEDGEMENTS

It was almost impossible, in the writing of *Mosaic*, to discern between who to include and who not to include within these pages for the generosity that life has extended to me in the realm of friendship and family could never be fully captured in one book alone. Any attempt to introduce even so much as a composite character inclusive of the attributes of one person and the detriments of another would be in vain for these characters would do little justice in conveying the impact of all whom I have been blessed enough to have come into contact. Without further elaboration, without flourish, the people I have come to know and love would cease to reside in the depths of my being where they belong and remain only superficial flesh wounds, rather than the beautiful scars they are on my heart.

For not only are they the tesserae of *Mosaic*, they are also the glue that binds this tale together. But they are more than just glue. They are the metals, those precious, precious metals, used in *Kintsugi*, a Japanese mending practice in which an object that is shattered is not discarded, but repaired with a lacquer of gold, platinum, and silver after which the object, whole once again, is regarded as more beautiful for having been broken.

And so, like *Kintsugi*, these friends and this family are the golden thread that etches its way through *Mosaic* through each and every word, before and after each punctuation, and all of the spaces in between. And like the strands of gold that can be traced across this shattered glass, they have shined a light, illuminating my life with their love and like that night in China, they are the stars in my sky, the light that I seek when darkness has fallen; my constellations, my comfort, my peace. And like that day in Rwanda I now have only this to say to them:

Thank you. Thank you. Thank you. Thank you. Thank you. Thank you.

And Finally: THE RHB

Because this is the page where first she will look, this is where you will find her.

It was a decade ago when we met in spin class. She sat to my left and by my side she has been ever since. For the last ten years barely a day has gone by where we have not spoken and, aside from my parents, she is often the first person I speak with in the morning and the last before sleep at night, as well as all of the hours in between.

Explanations for our friendship can be proffered in that we were both born in the year of the monkey and that we are both Virgos, so very similar in ways incomprehensible to those not born under our sign. But I know that our friendship goes back further than even the oldest stars in the sky.

The most generous of creatures, she has offered courage where there was fear, hope when there was despair, laughter where there were tears, and light when there was darkness. She has also entrusted me with her most precious gifts of all: her time, her patience, and her love.

If not for her *Mosaic* would never have been written. For, if not for her, my pen would never have found the page. For it was when my heart fell silent and my will grew weak that she was the one who whispered:

KEEP GOING

In Celtic, there is a word for someone such as she: *Anam Cara,* which, when translated means Soul Friend. The Celts believe that: "If you have been blessed by such a person in your lifetime, you have arrived at that most sacred place- Home."

So thank you, Christine Suppa-Hoyt, for being my home, my heart, my dear dear friend.

You are my unicorn and I will always believe in you as much as you have believed in me.

I love you more. I love you most.